RK Kliebenstein's Dedication

First and foremost, I want to thank God for the stamina, energy and knowledge he has blessed myself and the entire team of professionals it took to get this book to print. Without Him as a partner, this work would never have been completed, and to God, I give the Glory!

My co-author Jennifer was also a Blessing. Her patience, dedication and expertise enabled my ideas to come to life. Her tireless hours of editing and proofing are what made this work literate. Her publishing and marketing expertise is clearly a great contribution to the book. A special note of appreciation for Pastor Brian Burke who spent countless hours in layout and design, his talents are clearly evident in this work, and Saloni Punjabi who was also a blessing as she proofed and edited into the "wee hours of the morning."

My wife and business partner, Lorraine, has stood by me and urged me to persevere in getting a raw manuscript ready for edit by Jennifer. She motivated me to compile my thoughts and get them in writing, which frankly, without her, it would be three of four more years, if ever, for this to get to print.

This work is also possible because of the professional team at Coast-To-Coast Storage; Lorraine Kay, Bob Copper, Bob Vamvas, Margaux Voris and Carl Cunningham, who sacrificed to give me the time to devote to writing. The clients of our firm provided the capital for publication and marketing. To my friend and co-author Scott Duffy, of the first book "How To Invest In Self-Storage" for showing me that writing a book IS possible! The Virgo Publishing - Inside Self-Storage magazine folks will make this work a success with their support and marketing. A special thanks to Troy Bix, Jenny Bolton and Teri Lanza at Virgo for their confidence and support.

Last and never the least, this work is a product of the professionals in the self-storage industry. They are the genesis of each idea, thought and strategy. Without their innovation, dare to be different attitude, and their willingness to share, this would not be possible. A special thanks to Michael Gerber of the E-Myth, for allowing me to enter my Dream Room, where I could take all my ideas and those of my peers, and visualize them in print form. He convinced me to work ON my business, not IN my business long enough for this to come to fruition.

Folks, it is back to work to deploy these strategies and learn new ones. I hope you will contact me with your ideas and thoughts via e-mail at rk@askrk.com. I hope by now you've already purchased a copy of "How to Make MORE Money in Self-Storage", and if not, at end of the book is a special gift for you. There are at least two more books swirling in my brain…it is back to work and then off to the dream room!

How to Make Money in Self-Storage

Keys to Unlocking Self-Storage Profits

By RK Kliebenstein
& Jennifer LeClaire

How to Make Money in Self-Storage,
Keys to Unlocking Self-Storage Profits

ISBN-13: 978-0-9815126-0-0

Copyright © 2008

Published by:
Coast-To-Coast Communications & Publications, LLC
533 Muirfield Drive
The City of Atlantis, FL 33462

www.H2MMM.com

01 02 03 04 05 06 07 ¨ 07 06 05 04 03 02 01

No part of this publication may be reproduced, stored in a retrieval system, or transmitted in any form or by any means, electronic, mechanical, photocopying, scanning, or otherwise, except as permitted under Section 107 or 108 of the 1976 United States Copyright Act, without the prior written permission of the Publisher. Requests to the Publisher for permission should be addressed to the Permissions Department, Coast-To-Coast Communications & Publications, LLC, 533 Muirfield Drive, The City of Atlantis, FL 33462, Call: 877 622-5508, or e-mail: publisher@askrk.com.

Jennifer LeClaire's Dedication

I give all the glory to God for this book, and I'd like to thank RK for inviting me to join forces with him on this work, which I believe, along with the second edition, will serve as a sort of bible for industry operators. I've never met a man who is more knowledgeable about self-storage and I have learned a tremendous amount from him about the industry, as well as business in general.

I'd also like to give honor to my spiritual leaders and mentors, Jonas and Rhonda Clark, and special thanks to my precious daughter Bridgette for sacrificing a few Saturday afternoons along the way. My leadership team at Self Storage Promotions was a tremendous help during this process, keeping the operations running smoothly so I could focus more attention on this vital project.

CONTENTS

FOREWORD..1

SECTION ONE - GENERATING MORE REVENUE...................3
INTRODUCTION...5

CHAPTER 1 RENT
Rent: The Money-Making Foundation..7
Don't Confuse Occupancy with Revenue..8
Price Your Product Competitively...10
Keep Rates Abreast of Prices..13
Definitions: The Three Types of Rent..13

CHAPTER 2 ANCILLARY INCOME
Understanding Rents and Ancillary Income.....................................17
Rent Versus Ancillary Income..18
Making Money with Outdoor Advertising.......................................19
Understanding Your Placement Options..20
Selling Permanent Easements..21
What You Need to Know about Negotiations.................................22
Managing Ancillary Income Streams..24
How Ancillary Income Impacts Financing.......................................25

WWW.SELFSTORAGEPROMOTIONS.COM

SECTION TWO - EXPENSES......27
INTRODUCTION......29

CHAPTER 1 ADMINISTRATIVE AND OFFICE......33
Gaining Control Over Asset Recovery Expenses......34
Uncontrolled Supplies and Services......36

CHAPTER 2 ADVERTISING/MARKETING......39
Advertising Versus Marketing Versus Public Relations......40
Let Their Fingers Do the Walking?......41
But I Just Can't Do Without the Yellow Pages!......43
Selecting the Right Sized Ad......48
Getting the Biggest Bang for Your Yellow Pages Buck......48
The Multiple Book Dilemma......50
Saving with E-Commerce and Internet Marketing......51
Design a Customer-Friendly Site......52
Make Your Site Design Work......56
Start Tracking Today!......57
Keywords Enhance Listings......59
Develop an Online Customer Service Plan......63
Differences Between Online and Traditional Customer Support......63
Advantages and Shortcomings of Online Customer Service......64
The Essential Components of Online Customer Service......65
Manage Customer E-Mail......66
Posting an FAQ List......70
Identify the Most Frequently Asked Questions......70
Post Your FAQ Strategically......71

CONTENTS

Use Standard FAQ Formatting...71
Update Your FAQ Periodically..72

CHAPTER 3 INSURANCE

Risk Management: The Key to Insurance Savings.......................73
Advice from the Insurance Pros...74
Money-Saving Tips for New Construction.................................76
Tenant Insurance: Should I Offer It?...77
Surveying Special Situations..78
Seismic Risk – It's Not Just for California Facilities....................80
The Threat of Terror..81

CHAPTER 4 MAINTENANCE AND REPAIRS

Managing Maintenance & Repair Expenses...............................83
Disrepair as a Sales Barrier...84
Quality Control Commitment...85
Low-Maintenance Curb Appeal...87
Maintaining Resident Apartments..89

CHAPTER 5 MANAGEMENT FEES

Managing Management Fees...91
Set-Up and Lease-Up Considerations..92
The Value-Added Management Company.................................93
When It's Time to Sell the Property, This Making Money Strategy Really Pays Off...94
How to Select a Fee Management Company..............................95
A Laundry List of Possibilities...97

CHAPTER 6 SALARIES, PAYROLL & EMPLOYEES

Saving through Employee Training..103
Setting the Stage for a Lifetime of Learning.....................................104
Training: Getting Off on the Right Foot..106
Self-Storage Boot Camp..107
On-the-Job Training Tasks...108
When You Hire from the Competition..110
Executing the Ongoing Training Program......................................113
Seeking Specialty Training...115
Trade Shows, Seminars and the Internet...116
Payroll & Burden: A Sensitive Matter...118
Should You Use a PEO?..120
Employees Versus Independent Contractors..................................121
Exempt Versus Non-Exempt Overtime Classifications..................122

CHAPTER 7 TAXES

Saving on Your Taxes..125
Tax Savings Strategies: Cost Segregation.......................................126

CHAPTER 8 UTILITIES

Saving on Utilities: A Big Picture View..131
Conducting an Energy Audit..132
Check Your Current Electric Rates...139
Maintain Your HVAC Systems...139
Water Heating Issues..141
Indoor Lighting Considerations...141
Outdoor Lighting Options..142

CONTENTS

SECTION THREE - CREATING EQUITY AND VALUE..........145
INTRODUCTION..........147

CHAPTER 1 EQUITY AND VALUE
A Brief History..........151
Today's Self-Storage Markets..........152
Municipality Selling Points..........153
Where Do We Go From Here?..........154
Get Prepared for the Future Today..........155
The Changing Face of Storage..........156
Land Banking & Self-Storage..........156
First Generation Lessons Learned..........157
Cosmetic Surgery? Facelift or Collagen Injection?..........158
When Putting Lipstick on the Pig Just Doesn't Cut It..........160
Gleaning the Most from Your Feasibility Study..........162
Reviewing the Feasibility Study..........163
Going Back to the 1980s..........163
Pre-2003 Construction Considerations..........164
Design Standards & Site Configurations..........165
Up Versus Out..........166
Investment in the Property..........168
Capitalization Considerations..........170
Understanding the Sheer Economics..........171
Entitlements: Not a Good Reason..........172
Avoiding the Herd Mentality..........173
Market Research and Feasibility..........174
Making Lemonade Out of Lemons..........175

Dealing with Disposition..176
What About Relieving Stress on Management?.................177
Capital Gains Analysis..178
The Key to Disposition..180
Acquisition Analysis..181

AFTERWORD..183

NOTES...186

CREDITS...187

REFERENCE..189

ABOUT RK KLIEBENSTEIN..197

ABOUT JENNIFER LECLAIRE...199

FOREWORD

I often say optimism is a fundamental element of everything. Optimism gets you through the tough times, makes invention possible, drives all innovation, and is the lifeblood of entrepreneurs.

That holds true in self-storage as much as any other industry. That's one of the reasons I like this book.

"How to Make Money in Self-Storage" offers an optimistic view of money-making strategies in this real estate "play". From generating revenues to decreasing cap rates to cutting expenses, this book is jam packed full of practical – and proven – strategies for making more money in self-storage.

When I was on "The Apprentice" I found myself challenged in new ways, unlike anything I had previously experienced. Remaining optimistic was the driving force behind my success. I believe self-storage operators would do well to take the same approach in the self-storage game. Self-storage developers and operators are facing new challenges in an industry that has captured the attention of everyone from Wall Street to high-net worth individuals seeking to get a piece of this lucrative real estate pie.

I believe the difference between the winners and the losers in self-storage in the decades ahead will be found in the fundamentals – revenue generation, raising cap rates and reducing expenses – on a continual basis. I also believe the difference will be optimism to take the bull by the horns, so to speak, despite a handful of overbuilt markets, cyclical credit crunches, or the insatiable hunger of large institutional investors.

I encourage every owner/operator to pick up a copy of "How to Make Money in Self-Storage," read it from cover to cover, and then keep it on hand to refer back to from time to time. You won't find a better A-to-Z guide on all you need to know about profiting in the self-storage business. I intend to deploy many of the H2MMM strategies at Patriot Management, our family's self-storage endeavor.

So keep the passion, keep the optimism, and good luck to you in all of your self-storage endeavors.

Kelly Perdew
Season 2 winner of "The Apprentice"
Author of "Take Command: 10 Leadership Principles I Learned in the Military and Put to Work for Donald Trump"

SECTION ONE: GENERATING MORE REVENUE

Section One

INTRODUCTION

There is no greater way to impact the "bottom line" than to increase revenues. After all, the "top line" is where most of the impact to NOI can occur. Many operating expenses are not within our direct control, and in some cases, we may not have much choice in providers (read utility costs).

With income gain, we can directly impact the sources of income and create more revenue. The beauty of increasing rents is the long-term, multiplying affect. Compounding the gain creates exponential increases. Therefore, anything you can do to generate increased rent revenues from existing guests will have the greatest impact on your bottom line.

Here is an easy math calculation, demonstrating the highest affect of rent increases, after expenses, which enables you to make more money. Notice the difference in bottom lines. One would assume if you increase rents 10 percent, and your expenses are 25 percent, then the NET increase would be 7.5 percent (after expenses). NOT SO! It's actually 9.17 percent.

Old Rents	% Increase	$ Increase	New Rents	
$750,000.00	10%	$75,000.00	$850,000.00	
Old Expenses	% Revenue		New Expenses	% Revenue
$200,000.00	25%		$206,250.00	25%
Old NOI	% Increase (75% of 10%)	$ Increase (75% of 10%)	New NOI	Increased NOI
$550,000.00	7.50%	$56,250.00	$618,750.00	$68,750.00
	Anticipated NOI Increase (75% of 10%)	Increase Gain as %	Actual Increase	Increase Gain as %
	56,250.00	7.50%	$68,750.00	9.17%

Greater Gain 1.67%

Where this business really gets exciting is in the addition of new products and services. These are typically new streams of revenue, and, like box sales, these services can have a 100 percent mark-up. The exponential multiplying affect comes when you rent new space to guests that visit your facility to purchase the ancillary products and services you offer. This is where operators win big, and have really learned to make more money in self-storage.

Happy Learning and Earning!

Chapter One

RENT

THE MONEY-MAKING FOUNDATION

There are plenty of ways to make money in self-storage, but it all starts with rent. Since many of the other self-storage money-making strategies depend on ancillary income from tenants, having high occupancy rates is the beginning of greater profitability. In other words, if your facility is like a ghost town, then you are losing opportunities for additional sales of products and services.

Of course, there are two sides to the profit equation. The top line demands you to create income and the bottom line commands you to protect the revenues you collect from 'expense erosion.' Expense erosion is a failure to watch expenses that leads to a reduction in net operating income. These two core issues will be explored throughout this book.

Clearly, the money-making category killer is rental revenue. So if you had to choose a single area on which to focus your revenue growth endeavors – thank God you don't have to choose just one area, but follow us for a minute – then you would do well to focus on rental revenue growth as your number one effort. We're all looking for the return on investment, or ROI, right? Well, devoting more energy to rental revenue will offer you the highest payoff. A focus on rental revenue doesn't minimize the contributions revenue management can make in other areas, such as late or administrative fees, but it does have a multiplying affect that makes changes in other areas seem minimal. Here's the point: If you did nothing else to make more money in self-storage other than manage rental revenues, you would still make the largest possible impact on profits.

Are you ready to understand the underpinning of making money in self-storage by targeting rental revenues? Here are seven time-tested keys to lead and guide you on a journey to greater revenues and profitability.

DON'T CONFUSE OCCUPANCY WITH REVENUE

Confusing occupancy with revenue is a common mistake. Here's what you need to understand: Increased occupancy is

SECTION ONE: GENERATING MORE REVENUE - RENT

only a segment of revenue growth. It may be better classified as an indicator of higher revenues. Think of it this way: You can't collect occupancy, and it is very hard to spend. Occupancy must be converted to cash to be real. Your bank may care very much that you are 100 percent occupied, but the real barometer for making money in self-storage is what you deposit.

Many operators would erroneously choose to be "full" rather than "rich." So they keep rates low, do not raise existing guests to going market rental rates, and believe they are winning the game through 100 percent occupancy. Meanwhile, these operators are turning away callers and visitors that want to rent new space (which is now filled with lower paying guests). These callers and visitors are forced to rent from the competition and pay your competitor more than your current guests pay you. In the end, the mortgage payment, salaries, utilities, taxes and all other expenses keep on increasing over time while your rental rates stay the same.

The first step to making more money in self-storage through rent is setting rental revenue goals. When you set your goals, whether as part of the normal budgeting process or during an employee review, focus and concentrate on economic benefits instead of physical occupancy. Pricing your units is an important task. Considering the following areas is part of the formula for success:

- Inventory
- Occupancy
- Demographics

- Competition
- Quality of the Asset
- Salesmanship

When you set rental prices, the first point is to determine exactly what you are going to sell. If you have just a handful of 10x5s empty, but have rows of 10x10s empty, for example, you want to make selling the 10x10s your top priority. Always focus on selling the units sizes that tend to have the highest vacancy and highest inventory. As you set out to rent your units, be sure to understand the strengths and weaknesses of your store, such as amenities and location, and focus on the benefits of your strengths.

PRICE YOUR PRODUCT COMPETITIVELY

Here's a practical, money-making tip: Price your rental rates right behind your closest competitor whenever possible. If a 10x20 at the most expensive store in your area is $155, then, set your price right at $149.95. If it's not possible to price just below the competition – if the competition is low-balling the market just to fill up fast – then be confident about having the highest prices. Never apologize for being more expensive than the rest of the facilities in your area. If occupancies are very high in the market, then

SECTION ONE: GENERATING MORE REVENUE - RENT

set your street rates (industry lingo for asking price) higher than everyone else's.

What's the difference between pricing and rates, you ask? Good question. The answer is this: the maturity of the rental relationship. At ground zero, when a guest inquires about the cost of space at acquisition, it is price. After they move their goods into your unit and officially become tenants, the price becomes the rate they pay. Remember, adjusting price is different from adjusting rates. Prices can be used to test rates, and rates can be used to prove (or disprove) proper pricing.

Prices can be adjusted frequently – literally every hour in some cases. As soon as you achieve your occupancy targets, you should adjust your prices. This practice is known as revenue or yield management. It is a common strategy for airlines, hotels and car rental companies. You may have heard this technique referred to as commodity pricing. Whatever you want to call it, rest assured there is nothing wrong with tenants paying different prices for the same sized spaces.

Keep in mind, the only ones who may complain are the ones paying higher prices. However, as soon as everyone is paying the higher price, you can expect the complaining to stop. Revenue management requires good salesmanship, diplomacy, and common sense. Responding to complaints is a sales process, whereby you are simply re-selling the benefits of the space.

In 2002, Coast-To-Coast Consulting worked with a software company to establish the criteria for its revenue management program. It read something like this: When occupancy in size group "A" reaches "X" percent, prices are adjusted to "Z." When 10x10 size occupancy reaches 90 percent for 60 days, prices are increased by 2 percent. When 10x10 size occupancy falls to 80 percent for 60 days, prices are decreased by 5 percent. Simply stated, when occupancy reaches a certain percent for a certain number of days, the price is adjusted. Here is an example in chart form to help you see the formula:

ABOVE	BELOW
A 10x10	A 10x10
X=90%	X=80%
Y=60 days	Y=60 days
Z=2%	Z=5%

This demonstrates the purest form of supply and demand, when demand is high and supply is low, prices rise.

One of the effects of revenue management may be an anomaly in economic occupancy – values greater than 100 percent. This could occur when demand is high (perhaps at the height of a rental season) and supply is low (you and your competitors are at full occupancy). Then, a new competitor opens during the off season and occupancy drops, causing price drops (not rate drops). As soon as new occupancies strengthen, prices are again tested. Can you see the cycle? It's important to recognize and fully understand these market dynamics as you seek to make money in self-storage with rental revenue.

KEEP RATES ABREAST OF PRICES

One of the most difficult challenges is not to let prices get too far ahead of rates. The industry uses several different words to describe the prices you are charging new guests that rent from you. These are most often referred to as "board rents" or "street rates." When a caller inquires about the rental rates, this is the price you quote. The sum total of all spaces on the property at this rate – which is almost always the highest for units in that size category – composes your Gross Potential Income, or GPI. "Rents in place", also known as "actual rent" is what the renters are actually paying, reflecting any discounts they may have been given.

DEFINITIONS: THE THREE TYPES OF RENT

GPI Gross Potential Rents:	The sum total of all possible rents if 100% occupied 100% of the time
Board Rents or Street Rates:	The monthly charge quoted to customers for rents
Rent In Place (Actual Rent):	What the tenants are actually paying (after discounts or rent lag)

For example, Mr. Smith inquires today and is quoted $99.99, which is the board rent for a 10x10. Mrs. Jones, on the other hand, moved in three months ago, when a 10x10 rented for $94.99. She is paying the actual rent. The goal is to move Mrs. Jones up to the same rate as Mr. Smith within a prudent time frame. In high occupancy markets, where your board rents are slightly below the top of the market, the increase from actual rent to board rent might be a lag time of 90 days. In a market with weaker occupancies or where your store is charging top of the market board rents, the lag time may be 180 days.

The driver for this decision is how long it will take to replace a tenant in the unlikely event they move out when you raise the rent. There is nothing that mandates all size categories are on the same move-up schedule. If your 10x20 size is hot and you have a waiting list, then they should be on the shortest lag time. By contrast, if you have a "glut" of 5x5s, they will be on the longest lag time. It is important that the board rents and actual rents do not get too far behind one-another. When it comes to rent increases, the greatest risk for guest loss is when you raise the rent too much too quick. Guests will typically tolerate two small increases more easily than one huge increase. Where most operators get behind is they continue to raise board rents, but do not raise the existing tenants' rents. That causes the huge economic vacancy. When the lag becomes too large, it is often a lack of confidence more than a weak market that causes owners to have such a large disparity between board and actual rents.

How often should rents in place be raised? As a rule of thumb, not more than twice a year. If there is no difference between board rates and actual rates and the street rate difference is more than 5 percent, then consider a second rent increase.

SECTION ONE: GENERATING MORE REVENUE - RENT

Space	Size	Street Rate	Actual Rate	$ Diff.	% Diff.	When to Increase and how much?
#1001	10x10	$99.99	$95.99	$4.00	4.17%	$4.00 February 1
#1002	10x10	$99.99	$79.99	$20.00	25.00%	$10.00 February 1 & $10.00 July 1
#1003	10x10	$99.99	$104.99	$(5.00)	-4.76%	NO CHANGE

In any event, it is a good strategy not to raise rents for a new tenant until they have occupied the space for more than four months. Raising rents too soon or too steeply can cause strained guest relationships. Many managers fear raising rates will create vacancy. If you are out of a size category, then you have reason to celebrate. Your strategy then is to create a vacancy so you can raise the rate. Again, the fear of creating a vacancy is not a likely result of rate increases – unless they are severe or too often.

Many self-storage operators increase rents during their busiest rental season. But the better strategy is to raise the rent before the busy season begins. For example, if May and June are historically your two best rental activity months, then your rate increases should be in place for April. There are also other seasonal strategies. Some northern operators, for instance, raise rents in January because they are betting people will not move out when it is cold or snowing. There may be some strong logic here, but I would encourage you to consider moving up rates when you have the best chance of replacing drop outs.

One final caveat: The dirtiest word in storage is discounting. It is the most feared; least liked and yet most tolerated practice in self-storage. Discounting is a tool to fill empty space. A free month's rent with a six-month contract isn't the worst compromise in the world. When used properly, it can serve its purpose with minimum damage. But beware of competing on discounts alone or you could wind up with a full house, but a red accounting ledger.

Chapter Two

ANCILLARY INCOME

UNDERSTANDING RENTS AND ANCILLARY INCOME

Before we get into the nitty-gritty of revenue generation strategies in the upcoming chapters, it's important to get an understanding of concepts such as rent versus ancillary income. The last chapter offered you a strong foundation on rent, which is the key money-making strategy for this income-generating property type. However, it's not all about the rent. Rent is not the only factor in self-storage revenue generation. Ancillary, or Other Income, has been largely ignored and greatly underrated in the past. Large institutional players have proven that focusing on revenues other than in the form of rents, is an important profit making tool in self-storage.

NOI is a metric you'll want to keep a close eye on because it is a key to greater profits. In short, if you want to make more money in self-storage, you need to understand how to maximize your asset management. Understanding these concepts will put you well on your way to boosting your top line - and your bottom line to boot.

RENT VERSUS ANCILLARY INCOME

Let's assume you have done a good job managing rental rates. Your cutting-edge software application has prompted you to keep abreast of inventory control by making walk-through and lock checks easy, and having an accurate assessment of available vacant space for rent and yield or rental rate management. Let's also assume the difference between your economic occupancy and physical occupancy is small, with economic occupancy rating slightly higher. Let's assume, finally, that economic occupancy is "net" after collections (actual money deposited and collected). That leaves us with fee collections, charges, or ancillary sales.

As an astute operator, we will assume you have good policies in place regarding fee waiver, i.e. you waive fees only in extreme circumstances. Your tenacious management of late charges and collection fees will likely offer the added benefit of controlling rent loss through theft. Operators who manage fee income are typically heavily involved in occupancy management and catch theft early in the process. Now, if all the assumptions we made earlier in this section are inaccurate, you've got some work to do to set your house in order. But if you are faring well with inventory control, yield management, economic and physical occupancy and fee management, then you are ready to focus on ancillary sales.

MAKE MONEY WITH OUTDOOR ADVERTISING

Hundreds of self-storage businesses across the United States have implemented Outdoor Advertising Signs ("Billboards") on their properties in order to raise rental income on the site. There's good reason for this. There is still a high barrier to entry in this market, nearly no cost to maintain the signage, and a steady, long-term source of income that most self-storage owners would treasure.

> **Here's the challenge:** Most owners do not even know where to start or the right questions to ask about obtaining municipal permission to erect a sign. Due to the complex nature of the business, the authors turned to the leader in the industry, Tony Lockridge of Lockridge Outdoor Advertising, to learn more about making more money in self-storage with billboards.

The rental fees a billboard company can pay is directly related to the quality of the road a self-storage site is located on, the amount of traffic that road carries, and the visibility of the sign. This yearly payment can range from $1,000 to $25,000 for each year if the facility is located on an interstate in a major city.

UNDERSTANDING YOUR PLACEMENT OPTIONS

There are several strategic placement options for a billboard on a self-storage property. Many times the structure is near the road in the required landscaped portion of the property along the property line. Other installations have included installing the pole in between storage spaces on the outside next to a building. Still other properties, in order to house the billboard and collect the fees that come along with it, have decided to give up a small storage unit and place the poll inside the unit.

Here's some more good news: Billboard signs are now built on a single pole that is normally two to four feet in diameter. That means you won't need much ground space on your property to accommodate the sign. Consider the possibilities. Renting a storage space would net $300 per year and the billboard lease may be worth $5,000 a year or more (and never has a vacancy!) In summary, there are many areas on the property that work for placing the small pole that does not impair any appurtenant operations on the site. All you have to do is look.

SELLING PERMANENT EASEMENTS

There are yet additional opportunities for self-storage owners. Many property owners are now selling permanent easements to the billboard company for large, up front payments. The goal is often to raise capital prior to a sale of a property or to finance improvements. These deals can yield between eight and 10 years of up front lease payments. The billboard structure would then run with the land title, similar to power line easements.

Here's an example. Let's say a landowner is currently receiving $4,000 each year from a billboard lease. This land owner could instead negotiate the easement for $40,000 (ten years worth of income) to sell the rights to the easement to the billboard company. The lease would then end and the billboard and easement would remain permanently. For his part, the owner quickly raised $40,000 for two feet of ground space along a lotline that is out of the way of development.

If you are considering selling your property, it may make more sense to keep the monthly payments. At a capitalization rate of seven percent, the $4,000 annual payment is worth $57,142.86. You should also check with your accountant to see if the receipts would be taxed as ordinary income if earned during operations, or capital gains (1031 deferrable) taxable if included in a sale. All the income a commercial property generates, factors in on the valuation.

Can you see why many developers insist on finding properties with billboards? Outdoor Advertising offers a steady stream of income to serve as a backstop against vacancies or other operational pressures of the site. In other words, the addition of a billboard increases your property value.

WHAT YOU NEED TO KNOW ABOUT THE NEGOTIATIONS

Generally, billboard companies pay leases on a percentage of estimated gross revenues that the sign brings in. The industry average is approximately 15 percent of the gross revenue the sign generates. Payments can also be structured to increase over time due to inflationary pressures. The billboard company handles all permitting, installation, operation, and utilities. The only responsibility of the self-storage owner is receiving the yearly rent.

Of course, you'll need to offer the billboard company access to the property during business hours in order to periodically change the advertisements. On average, this occurs every six months. However, there is no heavy equipment brought on a site after the installation. Here's more good news: As a self-storage owner, you are indemnified

SECTION ONE: GENERATING MORE REVENUE - ANCILLARY INCOME

of all liability during installation, operation, and removal of the sign throughout the lease period. A current certificate of insurance from the billboard or sign company should be kept on file.

Permitting these signs are very difficult, and it truly pays to work with a company that knows the process and can create the materials necessary for municipal approval. There are many local, state and federal laws that govern billboards. The ability to place a sign on the property can depend largely on zoning, distance from other billboard signs, distance from residential areas, height restrictions, and many, many other criteria that must be applied to the site.

Because outdoor advertising is an income generator requiring specific zoning and permitting skills and experience, Coast-To-Coast and the authors have chosen to work with Lockridge Outdoor Advertising, which is currently the largest independent billboard development company in the United States. Lockridge has developed over 2,500 billboards. We chose a full service provider that handles the site evaluation, leasing, permitting and erection of these signs. If you are interested in reviewing your property for a billboard, please contact RK Kliebenstein at Coast-To-Coast Storage to prequalify your site and position you for making more money with outdoor advertising on your site.

MANAGING ANCILLARY INCOME STREAMS

Maximizing performance of an investment is the key to asset management. Most institutions, such as investment bankers, analysts, rating agencies, and publicly-held companies, consider asset management the highest level of good stewardship, a notch above property management.

While most self-storage operators do not draw a line of distinction between asset and property management, let's consider an asset manager as one who focuses on value creation, not just revenue growth. To that end, the asset manager must be cautious not to create such huge ancillary income streams that appraisers discount them in the valuation process. Huge ancillary income streams – that exceed 20 percent of revenues – present a challenge that appraisers and investors are forced to address.

Let us explain. Because one of the three approaches to value is the income approach, appraisers lean toward conservativeness and often cap ancillary income. That's because ancillary income is not produced by the real estate asset, but rather by management or business activity. Some of us see the day when a self-storage appraisal will have two elements of value, one as real estate and the other as a viable business entity. There will be a capitalization rate based on real estate and a value based on "X" times gross. This second method is how appraisers value retail businesses that do not have underlying real estate as a component of ownership. It's also how service businesses selling their "book of business" are appraised.

HOW ANCILLARY INCOME IMPACTS FINANCING

Ancillary income streams that are too healthy can also impact a project's financing. Ronald Pope of Wells Fargo had this to say about ancillary income exceeding 20 percent of revenues: "Our group would look at ancillary income at those higher levels, if there was a good track record from past history or strong contracts accompanied with a strong feasibility study supporting the market need. We typically will use 3 percent to 7 percent gross sales from ancillary sources. As always, we would listen to the 'story' and build the case from there."

So, if there is a potential penalty for increasing revenues, why concentrate on such activities? One reason is because you believe that someday self-storage valuation will be changed to account for strong ancillary income. The second, and perhaps best reason, is for the enjoyment of increased cash flows, even if the value does not increase commensurately. The third reason is to ensure full engagement of the assets. If your location meets most modern standards, your property may be classified with a highest and best use as retail instead of self-storage. Many self-storage sites today rival Wal-Mart, Home Depot, or car dealership locations. Just look at the neighboring properties of a well located self-storage store.

Since the location is as good as a competing retail location, take advantage of the traffic counts and add profitability to the store. Since the location is retail in nature…create a retail sales component within the property to justify the high cost and value of the land.

SECTION TWO: EXPENSES

Section Two

INTRODUCTION

Of the three paths to making money in self-storage, we have the least power to control expenses. But don't get discouraged. There are things we can and should do, and we'll discuss those initiatives in this section.

Here's a quick overview: Typically, expenses in self-storage operation are broken down into somewhat standardized categories, including administrative and office, advertising and marketing, insurance, maintenance and repairs, management, salaries, payroll and employees, taxes and utilities. If you want to control expenses in any or all of these categories, it's vital to measure them carefully and track your progress. The good news is most common accounting software applications such as Quickbooks® or Peachtree® have easy-to-create and manage Charts of Accounts. We suggest you set up the chart of accounts in the expense categories we've listed above, and then break the categories down in greater detail. At the end of the book, for reference purposes, we have provided a sample of how you might break down the categories (See page 189).

Keep in mind that as important as it is to create good, measurable expense accounts, it is equally important to maintain coding consistency. Each check written should follow in the same account, and allocations should be consistent. Phone bills present a unique challenge and therefore breed common errors. Here's why: Oftentimes, the Yellow Page ad costs will be billed with the monthly phone bill. But Yellow Page ad costs are not a utility expense (where we suggest you record phone expenses). Therefore, each month, the phone bill needs to be split up and allocated between the portion for Yellow Page (advertising) and for phone service (utility). Making matters even more complicated, some telephone companies also serve as your ISP (Internet Service Provider). Many of you choose to code your ISP and computer expenses to administrative and office category, which means yet another allocation of the phone bill. Since consistency is key to determining how much progress you are making, appropriate allocations are a critical factor.

One of the greatest cautions in expense management and dealing with vendors is to learn the difference between lowest cost and highest value. The lowest cost is not always the best value.

By organizing the three sections of the book (income, expenses and equity) in the same manner as operators keep

SECTION TWO · INTRODUCTION

financial records, it will be easier for you to organize your making money in self-storage strategies.

Chapter One

ADMINISTRATIVE AND OFFICE

In government and corporate circles, administrative and office expenses are often referred to as the "black hole." There's a good reason for that phraseology. Many businesses have let administrative costs get so far out of hand that a once profitable venture is drowning in the red. While this is an extreme and unlikely scenario in the self-storage industry, that doesn't mean we should ignore it.

If you want to make more money in self-storage, you need to get your administrative and office expenses under control. It's been said that if you take care of the pennies, the dollars will take care of themselves. We couldn't agree more. You could save thousands of dollars a year – and save a few trees along the way – by paying closer attention to this expense category.

Administrative and office expenses include asset recovery, such as collections and auctions, bank fees and card charges, office supplies and services, computer equipment, service and supplies, software purchases and support, data recovery and security, and ISP providers. Let's take these broad categories one by one and see how we can trim the fat – and save money.

GAINING CONTROL OVER ASSET RECOVERY EXPENSES

Gaining control over asset recovery expenses is not easy. It could be that there are only a few auctioneering services in your market. Or it may be that there are several, but only a few high quality outfits. What's more, government statutes may restrain your method of sale and you may once again find yourself stuck in a rut of limited options. In order to make more money, you may have to focus on the destination (results) rather than the journey (method).

> **Here's a few tips:** Make certain your auctions are timed properly, and do not create unnecessary auctions. Keep in mind that the cost of the advertising and the impact on your staff could be greater than the funds you recover in the auction. That's why we encourage you to settle every account

SECTION ONE: EXPENSES - ADMINISTRATIVE AND OFFICE

you can without a sale. If you can get a guest to pick up his goods and settle for a few cents on the dollar, it is preferable to an auction sale. Convincing the guest to pick up his goods relieves you of the risk of an improper sale. If you do offer to settle, the guest must vacate the space within a certain period of time as a condition of the settlement. In other words, if you are going to take a loss on the unit, get the tenant out. This is particularly true if the unit he is renting is a popular size or located in a prime spot at your facility. You can easily rent that space to a paying guest, so why compromise with a deadbeat tenant?

If you decide you have no choice but to auction off a tenant's belongings – or if you decide that the contents of the unit are worth enough to make it more than worth your while – then group as many guests into one auction as possible. This is often best accomplished by opting for first of the month rent due dates as opposed to anniversary dates. Whenever practical, guests should be offered easy payment options, allowing the guest to choose their due date (and then prorating). The first of the month due dates are "sold" at the beginning of the contract obligation, as it will be easy to manage the auction process if most rents are due on the first of the month. If a guest needs an alternate due date, you can accommodate them, but if they have no preference, then get as many rents due on the first as possible. Consider this script:

> "Mr. Smith, let's consider what day of the month you would like your rental investment due on. Most of our guests prefer the 1st of the month as it is easy to remember. Would that be convenient for you?"

If the guest wants an anniversary date or a specific date, we can accommodate them, and then 95 percent of the rents fall on the first of the month. (By the way that could just as easily be the 15th of the month).

UNCONTROLLED SUPPLIES AND SERVICES

Uncontrolled spending on supplies and services typically creates the "black hole" in administrative and office expenses. For self-storage operators, we can control expenses by watching supply costs. It is tempting for owners to provide managers with a Staples® or Office Depot® credit card as it makes it more convenient to purchase office supplies and it makes the store less dependent upon petty cash. The sheer convenience of a credit card may mean the manager makes more frequent trips to the office supply store, and is tempted to purchase impulse items, or shop without a list.

SECTION ONE: EXPENSES - ADMINISTRATIVE AND OFFICE

This uncontrolled, impulse shopping drives up office and administrative costs.

Most managers or customer service advocates will manage the daily expenses and can be conservative on supply purchases. However, when colored or gold paperclips are sitting pretty on the desk, when scratch pads are purchased rather than using scrap paper, and when bottled water comes from the office supply store, you've potentially got a less trustworthy manager on your hands. Helping the on-site team be conscious of saving pennies is a management issue, driven by example, and implemented through buy-in.

Here's a make-more-money tip: If you make supply purchases with Discover Cards or American Express, cash rewards programs can make more money for the operator by offering a rebate based on the percentage of your purchases. Other cards offer frequent flier miles, gas discounts or some other perks that could be to your company's advantage.

The cash rewards rebate, either as non-taxable (check this with your accountant) income in the form of a credit on your account (most cash rewards programs now issue checks), or the ability to choose personal items from a catalogue where rewards "points" can be spent, the dollar amount for single store office supplies may not seem significant. However, many years ago, I met a couple with multiple stores that purchased EVERYTHING (including their mortgage interest) that they could on a Discover card. The cash credit in one year was over $50,000. If you credited just $1,000 back to your expenses, the capitalized value at a 7 percent cap rate would be $14,285.71. So, even a very small saving can be significant.

Chapter Two

ADVERTISING AND MARKETING

From an expense control perspective, it's not really a matter of making more money in self-storage by reducing what we spend – although, we're sure to find some fat to trim out of the budget, if we measure our response. It's more a matter of getting the most value or the biggest bang for our proverbial buck. Stretching your advertising and marketing dollars, in other words, is the best way to reduce your expenses.

With that in mind, it helps to review the goal of advertising and marketing. Remember, the result you are trying to achieve as a self-storage operator is pure, plain and simple: guest acquisition. No matter what you do, or how much money you spend, or where you spend it, you need to keep track of how your activities help you increase occupancy. So while you might keep in mind increased phone traffic, increased walk-in traffic and brand loyalty, these measures don't go to your top line. You want to measure them because it is a metric of how well your advertising and marketing campaigns are working and could lead you to discover that your management is not closing the deal. But the ultimate measure of your campaigns is guest acquisition. In this chapter, we'll look at several of the most common marketing and advertising strategies for self-storage operators.

ADVERTISING VERSUS MARKETING VERSUS PUBLIC RELATIONS

Before we go any further, we need to spell out the differences between marketing and advertising, so you can isolate your spending under each category. According to the American Marketing Association (AMA), advertising is the placement of announcements and persuasive messages in time or space purchased in any of the mass media by business firms, nonprofit organizations, government agencies, and individuals who seek to inform and/ or persuade members of a particular target market or audience about their products, services, organizations, or ideas.

Marketing, by contrast, is the activity, set of institutions, and processes for creating, communicating, delivering, and exchanging offerings that have value for customers, clients,

SECTION ONE: EXPENSES - ADVERTISING/MARKETING

partners, and society at large. Advertising is one aspect of marketing, then. So is public relations, which the AMA defines as form of communication management that seeks to make use of publicity and other non-paid forms of promotion and information to influence the feelings, opinions, or beliefs about the company, its products or services, or about the value of the product or service or the activities of the organization to buyers, prospects, or other stakeholders. All three forms play a role in making more money in self-storage.

LET THEIR FINGERS DO THE WALKING?

Yellow Page ads are part and parcel of most of self-storage marketing strategies. In fact, some would say opening a brand new store in a competitive market without an ad in the Yellow Pages directory would qualify as a bona fide tragedy in the self-storage industry. How could you let this happen? Did you miss the insertion order deadline? Did the phone company forget to place your ad? Can you blame your marketing company? Was it sheer ignorance, or did you do it on purpose?

If one were to think way outside the box, you might be RK's partner, Bob Copper, President of Self-Storage 101. Bob did not put an ad in the Yellow Pages directory. Before you read on, be warned. Bob took a potentially high controversy position. It is important that you read this with an open mind. Some of you will say this is "crazy" or "insane." Others of you will say "gutsy" and "bravo" – someone finally stood up to the Yellow Page companies.

First, let's examine the rationale. Here is how Bob justifies his strategy:

> "I had a choice to spend money in the traditional form, Yellow Pages, where I would have a display ad lost amongst more than 100 other self-storage advertisers, or I could buy the biggest and best sign possible. I gambled on a calculated risk and won... big time!"

Here is what he did, or more specifically, what he didn't do: He did not place an ad in the Yellow Pages! We know, we know, we know. You skeptics and experienced operators are shaking your heads (as we did at first!). This strategy clearly works in limited situations, and is by no means the best strategy for everyone! But darned if it didn't work and make sense (and dollars) in this case.

Here's the brief history. 6th Avenue Self Storage unofficially opened in May 2007. The grand opening was mid June 2007. Both the soft and hard launch went off without a Yellow Pages ad. As of July 25, 2007, there were 126 occupied units. Bob rented over 140 units (The difference is move outs.) Exceptional? Absolutely. But the bottom line boils down to four strategies: location, location, location, along with leveraging the appropriate advertising and marketing methods to create guest acquisition opportunities.

BUT I JUST CAN'T DO WITHOUT THE YELLOW PAGES!

What if you feel you MUST use the Yellow Pages? What can be done to make more money? Consider the "five Ws and H" of Yellow Pages ads, i.e., the who, what, when, where, why and how of effective Yellow Page advertising.

When it comes to your Yellow Page ad, take our advice: Avoid being too artsy or abstract. The ad should be eye-catching and appealing, but most importantly it must speak to guest acquisition. Again, think like a journalist and make sure that the ad answers the following questions: "who, what, when, where, why and how?"

Let's start with "who." It's important that the shopper identify your store. If the shopper is letting his fingers do the walking through the Yellow Pages, then it's probably because they need self-storage. They just need a convenient, affordable facility like yours. The goal of the ad, then, is to motivate the finger-walker to choose your store over your competition. So make sure the name of your store is front and center. Make sure contact information is extremely easy to find. If consumers can't figure out quickly how to contact you, then they are likely to turn to the nearest competitor who makes their lives easier. If you have a web site, be sure to list that in your ad, too. The idea is to look at the ad through customer-colored glasses and make it easy for them to understand who you are, what you do better than the competition, and how to reach you in a flash. In most advertising, more is less. So don't clutter your add with extraneous information.

Now, on to "what." Since the shopper is already in the "storage" section of the Yellow Pages, you don't have to devote much space to the actual "what" of storage. There was a time when consumers were relatively uneducated about self-storage and its benefits, but that has changed over the years. They know what it is and why they need it. Now it's up to you to be the operator of choice in your area. If your unique selling proposition is climate-controlled space, then you may want to use that in your ad. If you have RV and Boat, mobile storage or records management, these would be noteworthy enough to mention in the Yellow Page ad, but if you have standard storage, similar to that of the competitors, do not waste much ad space on "storage."

So what about when? When do you place your ad? Well, we're glad you asked. You should place your ad in the Yellow Pages with a deadline that will coincide with your grand opening. In other words, you don't want to get out of the gate six months before you are open, but you don't want to be six months too late, either. At the end of the day, you are at the mercy of Yellow Page deadlines and may indeed miss the boat the first time around, unless you are aware of the

SECTION ONE: EXPENSES - ADVERTISING/MARKETING

close date (the date the directory stops taking new orders), and manage around the date.

Assuming you are already up and running, the "when" question becomes when to change your ad size. There are several factors to consider before changing the size, placement or text of your ad. One of those considerations is this: How well did your last ad perform? How much traffic did your ad send your way, and was it quality traffic or just time-wasting traffic? If you aren't seeing results from your ad, it's possible you have the wrong text, wrong design, wrong size or that you'd just do better off downgrading your ad to a free listing and spending your advertising dollars in another venue. If your ad is driving quality traffic in droves, on the other hand, then you may not want to change a thing - except for the size. You may want to run an even bigger ad!

Moving on to "where," you could take a couple of different approaches to making it easy for your would-be tenants to find you. Perhaps you've used a landmark-based strategy to distinguish your store, such as a line that reads "find us near the airport." Or maybe you even made the landmark part of your name, such as "Main Street Self-Storage" or "Airport Store & Lock." Whatever you do, make sure the address is easy to read. Make sure the landmark is common, keeping in mind that one of the primary reasons people use storage is because they are moving and they may not be intimately familiar with your market. Use major roads rather than retail store landmarks. The world is a changing place and if you are just north of the K-mart today, you may not be tomorrow.

You may even choose to include a simple map in your ad. The number one suggestion for making more money is to make absolutely certain that you have a map, however small, in your directory ad. This is the best way to answer the "where?" question and can be just as important as the physical address. Try to keep the map to three to five streets maximum. A clue below the address is always helpful, such as "next door to the post office" or "across the street from JFK High School."

So "why" should the customer choose your store? Be sure to communicate the reasons in your Yellow Page ad. This is called a Unique Selling Proposition, or USP. What sets your store apart from the as many as dozens of others running up and down the columns of the phone book? You'll have to make that determination by doing a little competitive intelligence. Visit the competing stores in your market, both from a distance/proximity basis and a positioning/amenity perspective. The USP ought to clearly differentiate your store from the competition. It could be the unit mix or the layout of the facility. If you didn't develop your store with a USP in mind, you may have to create the USP based on service offerings, such as free faxes, or a postal drop off center. Make sure the Yellow Pages ad succinctly highlights the USP. It need not be the focal point of the ad, but should hold a prominent position.

SECTION ONE: EXPENSES - ADVERTISING/MARKETING

Remember this: if your ad doesn't help the reader discern the difference between your facility and your competitor's facility in a few seconds, they may lose interest. But whatever you do, don't exaggerate or falsify a USP. Customers will see right through a thin USP. You'll lose credibility if you try to claim your facility is unique when you are merely a cookie cutter of your competition. For example, climate control is not a USP if there are other stores in the market with air conditioned space. However, if you have ultra-violet filters, you can claim something special and unique. Keep in mind that if your USP is simple and effective, your competitors may steal the concept (and vice-versa). Copycats erode the USP edge and may force facilities to find a new USP.

The "how" aspect of your Yellow Page ad deals with how they can pay. Depending on how much ad space you have and the complexity of the competitors, you may not want to even address this issue. Or you may want to use credit card logos instead of spelling out the card names. The easiest approach is to just say, "Credit Cards Welcome." The next aspect of the "how" is how the customer will get his goods to your store. That's easily accomplished with some bullet points that express "trucks," "convenient location" and "moving and packing services." Want to get an edge on the competition? How about a line that says, "Free pick up and delivery of your treasures"?

SELECTING THE RIGHT SIZED AD

Bigger is not always better in Yellow Page advertising. In fact, a two-page spread at the beginning of the section can be overlooked. Before you make a decision to go bigger, consider placing two 1/3-page ads instead. This strategy works if you are on top of the market rates and if occupancy is above 95 percent. If there is very little threat or presence of new competition, then try reducing your ad size. Multiple ads may require multiple phone numbers, and it is possible to use multiple ads to offer multiple USPs.

Beyond what we've already discussed, there are a couple of other issues to keep in mind when you are selecting the appropriate ad size. First, you may lose position, so if you like the position you are in, you may want to stay with the ad size you currently have. On the other hand, if a competitor changes the size of his ad, the page layouts could change and you may lose the position anyway. In other words, changing an ad size may influence the position of all the ads on the page – yours and your competitors. If you have poor position, changing ad size – even reducing the ad – may put you in a better position.

GETTING THE BIGGEST BANG FOR YOUR YELLOW PAGES BUCK

In some Yellow Page directories, you'll see placeholder ads that encourage you to advertise. Those placeholder ads are a clue that the directory couldn't sell the space. This is to your advantage. Most Yellow Page directories would rather sell that space than use it as a promotional tool. If you take the time to get to know your sales rep well, he may be willing to clue you in to the availability of those spaces before the book goes to print. This could be as simple as reserving your primary ad early and asking the rep to call you back at the close of the term with any "pick up" ads.

You can also try to force non-competitive ads. Here's how it works: Instead of taking a full-page ad, you would take a near full page and force the sale of a small, unattractive sized ad to a competitor. You should be careful with this strategy, but in very stable markets, we have seen a full-page ad reduced just enough to leave a low wide ad at the bottom, which is not as saleable or desirable. (Of course, that doesn't mean that a competitor will buy the space. The directory could choose to use it for its own purposes.) You might even choose to layout the Yellow Page ad yourself and see what ad variations would do. This is a very risky strategy because you have to be nearly 100 percent accurate or it can work against you. What if you end up with a competitor on the page? In most cases, the best bet is to play it safe and not try to gamble. After all, you could be on the receiving end of this strategy, forced to buy an ugly ad. You reap what you sow.

In some instances, upgrading to a color ad can land you a better position, or you may even get a one-year color upgrade free if you commit to a three-year package. There is typically a fair amount of flexibility in Yellow Pages ad sales, and some directories wheel and deal like a used car dealer with too much inventory.

Your ad may be eligible to appear in more than one category, particularly line listings. If you offer moving services, you may qualify for placement in the moving and storage section as well as household and commercial storage. An even more effective strategy is to appear in the truck rental category. If you offer pack and ship, you could also be listed in that section. Now you've got all your bases covered.

THE MULTIPLE BOOK DILEMMA

In addition to multiple categories, multiple book management could be an issue. Seasoned operators have the benefit of market research that tells them where high quality phone and foot traffic comes from. This information can direct the size and placement in your choice of Yellow Pages directories.

In some markets, particularly large markets, smaller, reputable directories are challenging the traditional Yellow Pages. These directories often offer a thinner slice of the local market and can therefore be user-friendly for consumers. Take caution if these books do not cover wide areas, however. It may not be necessary to advertise in more than one book if your trade area covers more than one market. In South Florida, for example, Palm Beach County is home to numerous smaller municipal communities. The main

SECTION ONE: EXPENSES - ADVERTISING/MARKETING

directory covers the 561 area code - all of Palm Beach County. A reputable directory company recognized the size of the 561 directory and decided to produce a smaller community book that divided the county. Unfortunately, those stores near the community splits needed to get into both books to get full coverage. The same would be true if you were on the edge of the coverage area between cities or counties.

Be cautious: There are some less-than-above-board Yellow Page directory companies out there. These companies offer books with very low circulation that sell ads that look, smell and seem just like the larger, more reputable books. Some of these books even run scams aimed at convincing you that you are renewing your existing ad, when you are really giving them your money instead. These directories often contact you through direct mail and time themselves to hit the market just prior to the natural renewal cycle.

SAVING WITH E-COMMERCE AND INTERNET MARKETING

Did you know there are more than 1,262,032,697 people using the Internet today? That number is growing year after year (day after day, minute by minute!), making the Internet the business platform of the future. In fact, it's already a major business platform today. It not only controls expenses by offering self-service and marketing savings, it can also generate big bucks for self-storage operators. The latter discussion may be premature for most facilities, but the expense control side of the equation is for the here and now.

Just think about it. Many businesses have gone global, thanks to the Internet-given ability to open a virtual store. Your storage facility may not need to go global since it serves a local customer, but leveraging the online channel can help you attract customers who may be moving to your area from all parts of the globe. You don't have to advertise in California, then, to attract consumers relocating from California. The same Web site that serves the self-storage reservation and payment needs of your local customers can also market to new customers wherever they are.

In this chapter, we'll discuss how to choose a domain name, how to design a customer-friendly site, how to improve your existing site, how to win natural search engine traffic, and a few online customer service skills that will take you a long way.

DESIGN A CUSTOMER-FRIENDLY SITE

Once you've selected a domain name for your site – we'd suggest something with the name of your store in it – then the next step is to design your Web site so that customers feel comfortable. That encourages them to stay on the site

SECTION ONE: EXPENSES - ADVERTISING/MARKETING

longer - a key to successful e-commerce. Remember, your goal with the site is to get your existing customers to make their payments online, and to attract new customers. It's also the perfect venue to advertise your retail products and your list of services to both sets of visitors.

Many Internet marketing and design principles are not standardized, and incompatibility between Internet browsers and programming languages abounds. Keep in mind that while browsing a Web site, the customer can't peer over the canned goods aisle to find the fresh produce section. So a user-friendly, easy-to-navigate site design is crucial to your success.

The cost of designing a site from the ground up can run from a few hundred dollars to millions, depending on the design features you choose. The truth is, because everyone is in the same cyberbusiness district, your plain and simple thousand-dollar Web site has just as much chance of generating solid profits for your small business as a million-dollar site does, if the design is customer-friendly. Buyers beware, though. You don't get much for $1,000 in today's market, and you can't buy into an online reservation system that's reliable for that price.

Consult with Self Storage Promotions for the most cost-effective solutions to your e-commerce and Internet marketing needs. In the meantime, here is a quick overview of your options.

No- To Low-Cost Solutions. You can build it yourself or you can use a turnkey solution to build a site for you. Building the Web site yourself is cost-effective if you don't include the costs of your time and if you have the necessary skills and energy. Choosing a turnkey solution will get you a professionally designed site for a small monthly fee, but you'll lose some creative control. Generally speaking, unless you have design and technical gurus in-house, we wouldn't recommend this option.

Mid- To High-Cost Solutions. Hiring a design firm or a freelancer, or assigning an in-house employee to design, and possibly to maintain, your Web site can involve major expense. Some tools, such as MS FrontPage, include templates that help you arrive at a competent design quickly, but they won't help you build your site's plan, a function called site architecture. Good designers cost from $50 to $100 per hour, which can quickly drive up costs if you're not completely sure what you're after.

Don't get trapped in your best intentions – the most common hazard on the Web. You want to make a good impression, but you also need to consider the basic demands of the Web, simplicity, functionality, and ease of use. Avoid these common pitfalls and you'll save time, hassle, and customers. Self Storage Promotions offers the experience and staff to give you realistic estimates and impressive results from your Web site. This is your chance to stand out from the pack, since most in the self-storage industry have poor quality sites.

Huge Sites. Beware of creating a site so large and unwieldy that changes will be troublesome. The design should lend itself to making simple changes to product information, for example, or adding a question in your FAQ section.

Inflexible And Un-Scalable Systems. Getting trapped in a proprietary system is perhaps the most probable danger. Flexibility is the key. Third-party hardware and rigid software systems can mean lost time and money for your small business.

Forgetting The Basics. Often, in the name of striving for a standout Web site, the fundamentals are left behind. Don't let amazing graphics and startling Web effects slow your site's download time and bore customers. To reach your Web site goals, you'll need people coming back again and again.

Ignoring The Competition. Check your competitors' Web sites for design ideas (what works, what doesn't work) and see how they apply to your site. Keep in mind that customers are likely to see their sites as well as yours, and with a comparative eye.

Thousands of vendors want to help you set up your Web site using their special expertise. To implement a customer-friendly site design, consider the following options:

Do-It-Yourself. The design of a competitive Web site from the ground up is a daunting task. It requires knowledge of HTML and perhaps other languages, such as Java. You'll also need to know about basic design elements and security issues.

Off-The-Shelf. If you don't want to learn HTML, you can use software such as, Macromedia Dreamweaver, Adobe GoLive, FrontPage and NetObjects Fusion that make site building easy. The next option level is the freelance designer. You can hire a freelancer for any degree of help, from advice to complete design. Or you can hire a design shop like Self Storage Promotions with a proven track record. Totally dedicated to design, these solutions have plenty of resources and experience. The level of service is up to you.

Turnkey Solutions. The turnkey solution can be expensive, but it takes a great deal of the decision-making off your shoulders. This solution will make proposals for the look and feel of the site; you pick the one you like and the turnkey program builds it with every feature you need. The program might also provide ongoing service and updates, for a fee. Self Storage Promotions offers these types of packages.

MAKE YOUR SITE DESIGN WORK

Your Web design evolves in response to company growth and customer needs. Measure the effectiveness of the changes you

SECTION ONE: EXPENSES - ADVERTISING/MARKETING

make along the way to make sure you are only making the changes that improve sales. Even simple daily changes, such as updating content and sales promotions, can have a big impact on the customer-friendliness of your site.

First, define a target measurement. In other words, what measurement signifies great design for your business? Increased traffic? Increased sales? Increased repeat visitors? All three? Some general factors to look at include changes in Web site traffic flow, the number of sales made, and customer response to design changes.

START TRACKING TODAY!

Design changes are made with a purpose in mind. For example, redesigning the order page is a change driven by the need to match shopping patterns. In this case, the redesign should facilitate the ordering process and decrease the likelihood customers will abandon the reservation.

If the number of reservations decrease or the number of questions about your facility increase after you've made a change, you need to find out specifically what your customers find difficult and rectify the problem.

Monitor Site Traffic. A favorite measurement tool on the Web, Web analytics reports supplied by your server's software or by your ISP can include such information as daily or hourly traffic volume, most requested pages, or error messages. In addition, referrer logs tell you where visitors came from and what pages they visited on your site. (Jennifer LeClaire also co-authored *Web Analytics For Dummies*, so feel free to contact us for more information on how to drive revenues using Web analytics.)

Measure Sales Volume Fluctuations. Though commonly used to measure the effectiveness of changes to site design, it might not be the most accurate indicator of a successful design. Many factors contribute to fluctuations in sales volume, one of which could be changes to design. Consider this when tracking the effectiveness of a design change, but use it in conjunction with other measurements.

Conduct Customer Surveys. Use online or e-mail surveys to elicit customer feedback. Remember the adage, "The customer is always right"? If you really want to know if something works in your site design, go straight to the customers.

A change in your site should increase traffic and facilitate flow from the product information section to the order area. Most important, sales should increase. Compare your data to previously established baselines or to target numbers established through comparison with similar sites. Relate customer survey data to sales information and page traffic. If the cost of the design change was greater than the increase in sales for a three-month period, the change was probably not worth the investment.

Based on the results of a cost-benefit analysis, decide whether to expand, maintain, reduce, or temporarily suspend your site design initiatives. You might need to consider a new designer or to hire one if you've been doing it yourself. You don't want to fix something that's not broken, but you do want to scout other vendors and rerelease your site with competitive features and functionality.

KEYWORDS ENHANCE LISTINGS

This chapter also promised a primer on saving money through Internet marketing. So without further ado, read on. You could spend an enormous amount of money on Google Adwords or listings on self-storage sites that let you post banner ads. We're not saying you shouldn't do those things. However, you can control your expenses by employing Search Engine Optimization, or SEO, strategies. SEO is the practice of designing Web pages so that they rank as high as possible in search results from search engines.

Most new customers find your Web site by typing a string of words into a blank box at a search engine. When your site comes up on the results page, they click on your listing. The trick to attracting customers is making sure your site gets listed high on the results to search engine inquiries. To make this happen, the first thing you'll need to do is identify the keywords customers use to describe your company and the services it provides.

You can take advantage of the handful of terms – keywords – customers use to describe your company and its services, such as "self-storage," "storage," "mini-storage," and your location descriptors. You should also leverage keywords that describe your amenities.

Choosing keywords is a great exercise in understanding the differences between offline marketing and online advertising. Once you've established effective keywords, it takes very little work to set up your pages and complete the submissions necessary to get listed on the top search engines and directories. The hard part is fine-tuning your entries, so that your site is listed in the first 10 or 20 results for the keywords that describe your company and its services. Again, you have a few options:

No- To Low-Cost Solutions. Find the keywords yourself; there's no substitute for knowing how your customers see you. Then you can deploy those words in your pages yourself or use some low-cost software to do it for you. You can also purchase low-cost software and use free or fee-based Web services to automatically submit your Web site to multiple search engines simultaneously.

Mid- To High-Cost Solutions. As the Web has grown, competition for a spot in the top 10 returns on most keywords has also increased. A growing battery of consultants and agencies is available to help you improve your ranking in search engine and directory results. These agencies charge monthly fees based on where in the rankings you want your site to turn up. Want to be in the top 10 in a competitive field? Expect a monthly fee of several thousand dollars. Be careful, though, there are a lot of scam artists out there.

The easiest way to get trapped is to cheat. With competition fierce for listing in the top 10 results with virtually all keywords, many people have found tricks to influence search engines in ways that search engine staff consider unfair.

So be warned: If you try these tricks, your Web site might be thrown out of a search engine entirely.

Outdated Software. Submission requirements for search engines change often. Using older site submission and search engine optimization software to submit your Web site, or to insert keywords into your site, might decrease your chances of getting good search engine turns. Also, some software packages use tricks that many search engines consider illegal.

Quick-Fix Solutions. Getting high listings is hard work and takes time. It typically requires rewriting your pages and manipulating your keywords to find the right combination of terms to get your site listed high on results pages. As a matter of course, quick-fix solutions usually end up as illegal entries.

If you know how much time and money you want to devote to getting listed on search engines and directories, you can narrow the choices rather quickly.

Build Your Own. If you're serious about your online business and have a marketing person dedicated to exploiting online markets, then you might consider bringing this expertise in-house. Weigh the increased traffic and sales against the cost of labor to determine the effectiveness of this approach.

Off-The-Shelf. There are several good software products that keep up-to-date on the latest changes to search engine submission requirements. These solutions, sometimes software-based, sometimes Web-based, will help you monitor and fine-tune your keywords and resubmit them to search engines. These programs typically cost several hundred dollars.

Turnkey Solutions. You can hire a qualified consultant who can maximize your returns quickly. For companies in the consumer market, where competition is most fierce, this might be a cost-effective alternative. Weigh the increased traffic and sales against the cost of outsourcing to determine the effectiveness of going this route.

Your first step is to brainstorm with your marketing staff and query your customers to see what words people currently use to find your site.

SECTION ONE: EXPENSES - ADVERTISING/MARKETING

DEVELOP AN ONLINE CUSTOMER SERVICE PLAN

Before developing your online customer service plan, it helps to understand the differences between online and offline customer support, the advantages and disadvantages of an online customer service program, the importance of keeping up with customer expectations, and the elements that every online customer service plan should include.

DIFFERENCES BETWEEN ONLINE AND TRADITIONAL CUSTOMER SUPPORT

Since the world of e-commerce is largely an impersonal culture, with virtually no face-to-face contact with customers, customer support enters a whole new dimension. Online, you must do things that you wouldn't need to do in the brick-and-mortar world, such as:

- Offer customer-friendly site design and navigation.
- Give sales transactions a personal touch, even though you may never speak to your customers.
- Ensure that ordering instructions are clearly outlined on your site.

- Answer questions and confirm orders electronically.
- Provide assurance of security of personal information transmitted over the Web.

ADVANTAGES AND SHORTCOMINGS OF ONLINE CUSTOMER SERVICE

Overall, the Internet allows you to make it easier for customers to do business with you because they can do it right from their desktop, any time of the day or night. While online customer support is certainly different than the traditional method, there are some distinct advantages:

- Lower customer handling costs.
- Improved efficiencies due to the use of posted ordering instructions and Frequently Asked Questions (FAQ) lists.
- Increased rate of customer retention if you make online shopping easier and more convenient than real-world shopping.

On the other hand, there are some shortcomings associated with virtual customer service that you should be aware of:

- Your relationship with customers will be less personalized because of the nature of online shopping, and they may have greater expectations of you as a result.
- There's a higher learning curve for your staff as they learn to deal with customers in the virtual realm.
- You'll need to make investments in expensive technologies and software solutions that aren't needed in the offline world.

THE ESSENTIAL COMPONENTS OF ONLINE CUSTOMER SERVICE

While every e-commerce site's customer service plan is, and should be different, there are some features that should be staples. They include:

- Web-based facets, such as simple navigation and design, fast image download times, and fast access to information.
- Human facets, such as quick e-mail responses, customer service phone numbers and offline purchasing assistance from customer service representatives.

- Product information, such as descriptions, specifications, pricing, FAQs, bundling, smart shopping carts, and cross-purchasing suggestions.
- Incentives, such as a free rental truck or a discount on packing supplies.
- Trust factors, such as explanations of secure transactions, information regarding privacy of data collected, branding (company logos and slogans), and endorsements by and/or membership in the Better Business Bureau, professional associations, etc.
- Fulfillment follow-through, such as confirmation e-mails and e-mail satisfaction surveys.

MANAGE CUSTOMER E-MAIL

On the information super-highway, e-mail is the primary connection between you and your customer. It offers the customer direct, fast, and reliable contact with your Web site. It can help you personalize the customer's experience, provide top-notch service quickly and efficiently, and serve as a precisely targeted marketing tool. Managed well, e-mail not only provides a window into your facility for your customers; it also gives you a window into your customers' needs.

The time and cost of managing your e-mail communications will depend largely on your system's design. If initial costs are kept low and the system produced is simple enough to accommodate staff turnover, return investment on e-mail management can be immense. Some software manufacturers claim that enhanced e-mail management results in up to 100 percent improvement in customer e-mail response and significant improvement in repeat sales.

No-Cost Solution. Many companies have created excellent e-mail management systems based solely on their Web site's ability to pop up e-mail windows in their customers' e-mail client programs. However, these systems require disciplined internal habits to ensure that each e-mail message receives its proper response.

Low-Cost Solutions. Off-the-shelf e-mail response software can cost anywhere from $49 to $30,000. Low-end systems can provide some fundamental technology to help you respond to each e-mail message as well as to organize, save, and track trends in your e-mail correspondence.

Mid- To High-Cost Solutions. These solutions typically integrate e-mail correspondence with other customer service efforts and are written to handle high traffic volumes reaching thousands of e-mail messages a day. These systems might integrate with call centers, online chat, or direct-mail efforts.

As you get into the high-end e-mail management systems, there's an increased risk of getting caught in your vendor's system. Three factors to evaluate when choosing a vendor are:

Storage Systems. Most systems use common formats to save e-mail that can be easily converted to another e-mail system. Be careful not to lock your e-mail history in a system that can't be converted to another form if you choose to switch vendors.

Back-End Integration. If you're connecting your e-mail responses to other customer service efforts, make sure the two systems are compatible. If not, you might have to consolidate your customer service efforts under one vendor.

Hardware Requirements. Make sure any required hardware is compatible with your other systems and that you can move the data to another system if you choose.

Flexibility And Scalability. Before committing to a system, be sure to ask about flexibility and scalability. A common mistake of many small e-businesses is outgrowing a system before it has paid for itself. Keep your growth goals in mind when choosing any component of your information technology infrastructure.

How you initially set up your e-mail system will depend upon whether you select a build-your-own, off-the-shelf, or turnkey solution.

SECTION ONE: EXPENSES - ADVERTISING/MARKETING

Do-It-Yourself. Clearly, the do-it-yourself route will take the most time and will depend on your programming abilities. Unless you are developing a highly specialized proprietary system, chances are you'll be better off purchasing ready-made software.

Off-The-Shelf. The e-mail program was the first program written for the Web; programmers have been churning out e-mail management systems ever since. The off-the-shelf option boasts a variety of systems that range from $49 shareware to complex systems costing $30,000. The functionality of these programs is widely different, with the more expensive versions providing an astonishing array of features. Off-the-shelf programs are often capable of same-day installation and can require anywhere from a few hours of training up to a six-month integration scheme.

Turnkey Solutions. Generally, these systems are highly customizable and capable of integrating snugly with your database, shipping, and management software systems. They are complex and usually require training personnel to use the software and to maintain the system.

To many Internet users, a late response is worse than no response at all. Confirming receipt of all incoming e-mail messages is the first step toward earning the trust of your online customers. But that's just the tip of the iceberg. Understanding how to use e-mail effectively will increase your company's chances for positive interaction with customers – and positive numbers.

POSTING AN FAQ LIST

To begin building your frequently asked questions (FAQ) list, you will first need to gather a list of commonly asked questions. Once this has been done, you can create the list, keeping in mind that an effective FAQ has several important characteristics: It is posted strategically, uses standard formatting, and is updated periodically.

IDENTIFY THE MOST FREQUENTLY ASKED QUESTIONS

To compile a comprehensive list of frequently asked questions, begin by talking to your staff on the front lines of customer service. Ask the people who answer the phones which questions (and objections) they hear most frequently. Look through your e-mail to find customer inquiries that might apply to most of your customers. Finally, ask other staff members to brainstorm about questions customers are likely to have and add them to your list.

Questions typically found on a good FAQ list are those involving:

SECTION ONE: EXPENSES - ADVERTISING/MARKETING

- Pricing.
- Which payment forms are accepted.
- Privacy policies regarding credit cards and other sensitive information.
- Shipping and return policies.

POST YOUR FAQ STRATEGICALLY

Post a link to your FAQ list in a visible section – preferably on several different pages – of your site. If customers do not quickly see an FAQ link, they may send redundant questions to your service center – or worse yet, log off of your site - defeating the entire purpose of this important feature. You might want to have more than one FAQ. For example, you might want to have one for customer service questions, such as those about reservations, and another focusing on product issues.

USE STANDARD FAQ FORMATTING

Begin by listing the questions at the top of the FAQ page, with individual hyperlinks that lead the customer to the questions and full answers below. (This HTML technique uses the <A name=NAME> tag to place a target next to the answer to the question within the FAQ and also to make the listing of the question at the top of the FAQ into a hyperlink.)

As your list grows, you can group questions into categories to allow visitors to search through them more easily. At the bottom of the page, be sure to add an option for viewers to e-mail your customer service staff in case their questions weren't answered by the FAQ list.

UPDATE YOUR FAQ PERIODICALLY

Remember, an FAQ is a working document that should be periodically updated to reflect the most commonly asked questions. Some organizations maintain a call log to spot questions trends. E-mail correspondence leaves a trail of subject lines that can be helpful for identifying new questions. Every three months (quarterly), review your customer service calls and e-mail logs and post the new questions.

Armed with this information, you are prepared to rush online and make more money and save more money in self-storage with e-commerce and Internet marketing.

Chapter Three

INSURANCE

RISK MANAGEMENT: THE KEY TO INSURANCE SAVINGS

You know the old saying. Nobody appreciates the value of insurance until they need it. The truth is, you need self-storage facility insurance, even if you don't have a mortgage company to deal with. But there is another truth that you will like much better: You can save money on your insurance costs and add to your bottom line if you employ some time-tested strategies and sound wisdom.

Of course, the legal gurus warned us to "exercise great discretion and caution" in suggesting ways to make more money by reducing insurance costs, particularly with regard to coverages – both from a limitation and deductable perspective. So please allow us to set the record straight, right up front. There are risks, from natural disasters to mold litigation, and owners should be very careful with any attempt to create cost savings in insurance. If you employ the wrong strategy, it could leave you without enough coverage. Risk management is the name of the game.

With that said, we will discuss several strategies for making more money in self-storage by cutting insurance costs in this section. So read on, but be sure to balance our suggestions with the wisdom of your own counselors, including attorneys, accountants and insurance agents. While the information we share with you in this section is proven to work, every facility and every situation is different. You may even have other strategies to share with us.

ADVICE FROM THE INSURANCE PROS

Mike Voelz is a commercial property insurance agent for Bader Company, an insurance brokerage that offers policies from various insurers. He's seen plenty of different situations over the years and offers some good advice for saving money on insurance costs:

> "For an owner-operator, one of the most important things you can do to reduce the cost of your com-

SECTION TWO: EXPENSES - INSURANCE

mercial policy is to find an agent that you trust, one who works with you to find a policy that best fits your needs. There are several insurance companies in the self-storage industry that specialize in commercial policies designed specifically for self-storage. There are also some agents who can represent more than one company, allowing you to select from several quotes. Don't skimp on your insurance coverage. It is one of the most important decisions you can make for the security of your business and your bottom line."

When asked, are you paying too much for insurance? Randy Tipton of Universal Insurance responded with some wise counsel of her own:

"I am sure that every storage owner across the country would answer this question with one word – YES! While many of you have received excellent advice and have a well-written insurance portfolio, there might be ways to save money and improve your coverage."

The most material way to save premium and increase coverage is to take out your insurance coverage with a self-storage industry professional, or have your local independent agent represent your facility to the same markets. You might ask why...there's a good reason, indeed. The insurance programs that specialize in self-storage know your business and like it. The premiums reflect that affinity. Even more important, there are unique coverages that are vital in order to fully cover your facility from risk that you won't necessarily find in other industries. By dealing with insurance companies who specialize in self-storage, you can improve your protection and save money at the same time.

MONEY-SAVING TIPS FOR NEW CONSTRUCTION

If you are new to the industry and just considering building a facility, there are some tips that could save you some money before you even get started. Here's the first one: If that piece of land you are thinking about developing into a storage facility is in an area that doesn't offer protection from the local fire department, it could cause you some trouble when you attempt to secure insurance on the facility.

The property portion of insurance premiums is determined by many factors, one is the ability to quickly fight a fire. If there is not an acceptable water source, such as fire hydrants, on or near the property - and if they are not manned by a nearby fire department ready to fight the flames - you might meet with considerable higher than normal insurance premiums. Or worse, you might find that you are unable to obtain insurance at all.

What about construction and security? Your insurance professional will ask you questions relating to the type of construction. If you are building with metal, you will be asked about the metal gauge. The heavier the metal, the better the quality of the property. Higher quality properties may enjoy lower insurance premiums. A sprinkler system in the facility with full protection will also save you insurance dollars. Most self-storage insurance providers will offer lower premiums to facilities that have invested in protecting the property with state-of-art security.

TENANT INSURANCE: SHOULD I OFFER IT?

Some other considerations to think about are your lease and your knowledge of the business. The lease is an important tool for you and your insurance company in the event of a loss. Your insurance provider will typically review the lease with an eye toward certain, specific clauses. A limitation on value of tenant goods is also a valuable tool. You could also consider joining your state or national association and attend the educational trade shows that are available. All of these steps afford you an opportunity to convince your insurance provider that your facility is top-notch and worthy of best premium credits.

We highly recommend offering tenant insurance. It provides a service to your tenants and offers your facility an additional layer of protection. Some insurance companies will offer a credit on the Customer's Goods Legal Liability Coverage, if you offer tenant insurance. What's more, many of the tenant insurance programs offer a referral fee to you. To review, you get a premium savings and a referral fee all while offering a valuable, needed service and adding to your insurance protection. This is a must-do for every facility.

Talk to your insurance provider about premium savings for high deductibles. Understand the difference between a percentage deductible, a deductible per building, and a standard deductible. You might also want to consider insuring the wind exposure in a state wind pool and obtaining the remainder of the coverages separately. Before you call your insurance agent, have your ducks in a proverbial row. Know everything there is to know about your facility. The gauge of the metal, the wind uplift for the roof, the condition of the roof, and every aspect of security are important factors insurers consider when you submit your property for premium and coverage underwriting. The best properties will have the best chance to secure insurance.

SURVEYING SPECIAL SITUATIONS

For most of the United States, the standard policies written for physical damage insurance are sufficient. There are, however,

SECTION TWO: EXPENSES - INSURANCE

certain areas of the country that will require extraordinary coverage because of increased exposure to risks. Operators in coastal areas are still feeling the sting of years past. While there has been some increase in capacity and lowering of premiums, insurance availability and competitiveness is not available. In order to save money, you might want to consider a higher deductible. Then again, you may not have much of a choice. High deductibles are often a requirement in writing coastal properties.

The problem with hurricane-prone regions of the U.S. is two-fold. First, damage from 100-plus mile per hour winds is typical in even mild hurricanes. Second, flooding becomes an issue. As the tide surge rises, areas near the coast are directly impacted. In New Orleans, Hurricane Katrina demonstrated the importance of building a facility on high ground, in the wake of broken levies that left waterlogged buildings. The reality is most of the property damage was somewhat predictable in New Orleans. When the altitude of your property is less than sea level, it's a clear warning signal of the impending doom sooner or later.

It is a matter of risk. Since there had been no major losses in the lifetime of the developers, and more important, no claims made against insurers, the marketplace was satisfied that risks were very low. Some shrewd and conservative insurers did not insure this flood risk. Others allowed owners to self-insure. Because lenders were seeking high returns from loans in a very competitive space, they analyzed the historical loss/claim data and did not force many property owners to take out flood insurance. The rest of the story is, well, tragic history.

A standard flood insurance policy will cover structural damage, HVAC equipment, clean up of debris post-flood, and floor surfaces. Riders can be purchased to insure contents. The standard commercial coverages are $500,000 for a business structure and $500,000 for business contents. There are yet other special risks to consider, including seismic risks, terrorism, loss of income, and liability insurance.

SEISMIC RISK - IT'S NOT JUST FOR CALIFORNIA FACILITIES

Seismic risk, that is risk from earthquakes, is largely mitigated through proper construction techniques and materials. Seismic risk is not limited to California as many may believe. Like flood risk, seismic risk is found in any community located in an area with elevated terrain, such as a mountain, because it lies close to a fault. A fault is created as the result of some seismic activity – even if thousands of years ago when water may have covered the land. Seismic risk is not limited to earthquakes, either. If the land settles and ground shifts, then the structure could see damage – if it wasn't designed to tolerate ground movement.

In self-storage, the greatest evidence of possible seismic damage is a cracked drive surface, which is a fairly common occurrence over time. A self-storage project in Texas recently was listed for sale. A lender owned the project after the borrower defaulted on the loan. The buildings started to settle due to what was determined to be seismic activity, and the buildings were not insured against seismic risk. The units slowly became unrentable, first due to inoperable doors and then unrepairable drives. The income eventually dropped below the point where the owner-borrower could service the debt. He lost the property. The moral of the story is that seismic insurance may not only be appreciated in San Francisco or Los Angeles, but in the plains of Texas.

The misalignment of buildings, which causes doors to not operate properly, is a more common troublesome result. While some of these impacts may be cured with tension alignment, more severe cases require more dramatic repairs. If you construct your entire building on post tension slabs, the facility can better withstand these ground settlements. However, they are still susceptible to damage. Visit www.ShakyGround.biz for more information on the types of damage from seismic activity could cause to your facility.

THE THREAT OF TERROR

Before September 11, 2001, the risk of terror was seemingly small. Before 9-11, we could only reference the World Trade Center and Oklahoma City bombings as potential warning signs for the self-storage industry. In both of these tragedies, perpetrators relied on self-storage facilities and or truck rentals to help them accomplish their dirty work. Potential terrorism-related losses become much more prominent on 9-11, where damage is estimated at $31.7 trillion. Since 9-11, most casualty and property damage insurance policies for commercial real estate exclude loss from terrorist activities.

The TRIA (Terrorism Risk Insurance Act) was in place through December of 2007, providing for the sharing of private and public compensation from acts of terrorism and the subsequent insured losses. The nature of this Act is to create a more granular risk for insurers, noting that catastrophic losses are likely to be concentrated in a very small geographic area, such as the World Trade Center. The true key to managing the risk lies in the hands of local governments' ability to deploy crisis management programs. It has been said that $7 in losses are saved for every dollar spent on developing a Crisis Management Plan.

Chapter Four

MAINTENANCE AND REPAIRS

MANAGING MAINTENANCE & REPAIR EXPENSES

Just like administrative costs, maintenance and repair expenses can easily get out of hand. It's those little foxes that spoil the vine, but there are some big foxes to watch out for, too. Making more money in self-storage means controlling expenses both penny and dollar wise. In other words, we need to pay attention to the big and small stuff. Focusing on saving money on repairs and maintenance at the expense of not completing repairs can cost you far more money in the end.

Case in point: a metal panel in a humid climate or a wood rail in a high precipitation area that gets scraped. Failing to repair that scrape, seal and paint the panel or rail may lead to rust or wood rot. If that happens, you have a much more costly repair job on your hands. Even before we get into the nitty gritty of this chapter, let us say this: Don't leave roofs, water leaks, cracked driveways, asphalt breaches unrepaired. That's penny and dollar foolish.

Repairs and routine maintenance seem to be the one area of expenses that has the most cause-effect relationship. In this section, we'll discuss how to manage maintenance and repair expenses wisely so you can see greater profits rather year after year.

DISREPAIR AS A SALES BARRIER

Unattended repairs or maintenance in areas, such as the common areas could create a sales barrier. Consider the old adage, "You only get one chance to make a first impression." Trite, yes, but absolutely true. Try to look at the situation through customer-colored glasses. Now, imagine you are entering a facility with obvious maintenance issues on the sales floor. We'd liken the experience to taking a tour of a restaurant only to enter the kitchen and find roaches crawling about or mayonnaise stored at room temperature.

Cleanliness may not seem as important in a self-storage facility as it does to a restaurant. While your floors may not need to be clean enough to eat off, they do need to be as clean

SECTION TWO: EXPENSES - MAINTENANCE AND REPAIRS

as possible. Now take off your customer-colored glasses for a moment and put on your owner-colored glasses again. If your property is dirty, it sends a message to guests that it's OK for them to ill treat the property as well. If there's trash and cigarette butts lying around on the grounds, then that gives them unspoken permission to throw their trash on the ground, too. If you've got sloppy tenants, then your staff will spend more time cleaning up the facility and that could lead to lost rental opportunities. Good housekeeping sets a standard for guests to follow. Even older properties can be cleaned and well maintained.

Go beyond keeping the facility clean. Make sure the office and common areas are brightly lit and painted annually or more often if it's necessary. There is absolutely no excuse for dirty entrances, parking lots or sales floor areas. All trash receptacles on property should be emptied daily, particularly when rodent or pest attraction is possible. To make it easier, every store should have a daily maintenance schedule – better referred to as a "quality control commitment" list. The entire property should be walked and checked for needed maintenance and repairs.

QUALITY CONTROL COMMITMENT

Here's a quick checklist of items that should be part of your facility's quality control commitment for individual spaces. Each vacated space should go through a quality control process and be made "rent ready" before the staff shows it to a prospect.

- The floor should be swept clean and debris removed, including corners. Vacuums are better than brooms.
- Walls should be dusted or wiped down, free of sharp objects that protrude, and even Galvalume painted if necessary. Galvalume is a 55% Al-Zn alloy-coated sheet steel.
- Doors should be dusted and wet-wiped, inside and out.
- Doors should be lubricated and tensioners adjusted so they operate as well as they did when the store first opened.
- Latches should be lubricated. They should slide easily to demonstrate to tenants how they operate and secure the space. If the door needs adjustment to line up with the latches, the adjustments should be performed immediately upon either request by the guest or at the time the space is vacated.
- If there are lights inside the space, the bulbs should immediately be replaced as needed, and either energy efficient or low watt bulbs should be used whenever possible.

SECTION TWO: EXPENSES - MAINTENANCE AND REPAIRS

- If pest control or rodent control bait is necessary, it should be placed near the door rail, out of sight, and where it is easy to change. Extra bait should be available at the office so it can be exchanged in occupied spaces at the request of the guest or management.

After the space has been inspected for 100 percent quality control, you can document it and use it as a sales tool. A hang tag should be placed in the space. You can learn more about this in the section on audits toward the end of the book.

If proper examples are set for guest behavior, and ample opportunity exists for guests to properly dispose of trash, the maintenance impact on the staff will be reduced. Making a strong effort to communicate your expectations for cleanliness at the time the guest moves in, goes a long way toward reducing undue maintenance. Let your guests know that it is their responsibility to remove all debris and trash they create, and make them aware of property rules, and not to leave furniture or other large items by trash bins for disposal. This will reduce the need for dumpster space and help you save money on that front.

LOW-MAINTENANCE CURB APPEAL

Flowers and landscaping can make a property more attractive and create curb appeal, but a smart owner looks for low-maintenance solutions. Flower boxes can replace flower beds, for example, and using durable silk or synthetic flowers in areas where guests can only see the landscaping from a distance can reduce costs. By the same token, lawns and grass can have a cooling and soothing effect, but the bottom line is finding beauty in Xeriscape techniques as they can be more financially rewarding. Use potted plants among bark or rock and splashes of color to replace lawns, for example. When possible, large areas may use low-growth ground cover instead of grass.

If your parking areas are asphalt, they should be sealed regularly and restriped often. Parking bumpers should be painted quarterly or touched up more often if needed. Weeds are not acceptable under any circumstance. Cigarette butts from staff members are grounds for dismissal.

MAINTAINING RESIDENT APARTMENTS

When it comes to resident staff apartments, you should use an occupant agreement that places the responsibility for maintenance on the occupant, not the landlord. Occupancy agreements should allow for maintenance inspections annually, or for at any other time the owner feels it is necessary. Inspection should only be done in the presence

SECTION TWO: EXPENSES - MAINTENANCE AND REPAIRS

of the occupant. Seek legal advice for the proper wording of an occupancy agreement.

Whenever possible, a damage deposit should be collected from the manager occupant, $500 to $1,000 is recommended. Deposits, whenever possible, should be kept in an interest bearing account, with interest paid to the occupant. You could set goals for the return of deposits, however we don't recommend it. "You have to pay to stay" sends a clear message to staff members about your expectations. Your stringent rules and high expectations of acceptable behavior will transfer from the staff to the guests.

Using outside services for maintenance and repair is necessary in some cases. Work contractors should be held to reasonable and fair standards. Only use contractors that are licensed (when appropriate), bonded and insured. The contractor should carry its own workers compensation insurance, and certificates of insurance. These documents, as well as licenses, should be kept on file.

Chapter Five

MANAGEMENT FEES

MANAGING MANAGEMENT FEES

When it comes to management fees, making more money in self-storage depends on, you guessed it, management! And the answer isn't always changing management, either. Sure, there are some baselines that constrain us. The industry standard management fee is 6 percent of the revenues collected, with a minimum fee per month, during the initial lease-up. Still, it is possible to make more money in self-storage by managing management fees. So read on to discover some tips, tricks and tactics that will put money in your pocket and a smile on your face.

SET-UP AND LEASE-UP CONSIDERATIONS

For very large projects or higher than average revenue locations, you may indeed be able to negotiate a discount from the standard 6 percent fee. A discount may also be appropriate if the fee management firm manages multiple properties for the owner because they can streamline the operations at various levels. However, there are two areas we don't recommend trying to negotiate for the *sole* purpose of saving money: during set-up and during lease-up.

Before the grand opening, it is customary for your newly retained management company to charge a set-up fee. This fee includes services such as loading the door table into the software application – or straightening it out – staffing and setting up the office, working with the contractor to create or complete punch lists, and setting up the marketing tasks to give the project every opportunity for success. This clearly does not sound like a time to de-motivate the management company!

That said, you may be able to negotiate a rebate of all or a portion of this fee for continued employment of the management company. Realize the management company's biggest fear is that they will do all the hard work of getting your project to stabilized occupancy, and then be released from service just as the project intensity is lessened. Perhaps you could negotiate a rebate of 33 percent of the set-up fee after the first 36 months of engagement and the balance of the fee after the company's fifth year of service.

A management company's practice of charging a minimum fee of between $2,500 and $4,500 (fee varies based on the price of the facility) is customary and makes perfectly logical sense. There may be some room for negotiation, but operators should be cautious about cutting back during lease-up. This is the time in the life of the project where intense energy and attention to detail may be the most critical. Cutting the management company's fees during a period when they should be at the top of their game may be counterproductive in the short run and the long run.

THE VALUE-ADDED MANAGEMENT COMPANY

Management companies may be able to save you expenses greater than their fee if they can integrate your property into an existing Yellow Pages ad. This is most likely for a small property, or a property with phased construction, where the total number of spaces is smaller than a traditional or fully built-out self-storage property. If you could save several thousand dollars and get moved to the front of the book in a full page or double-truck[1] ad, and only pay for a portion of the ad, wouldn't that be terrific? Remember, in some directories just getting to a full page ad will get you moved forward in the book. It is a common (but not absolute truth) that getting placement toward the front of the directory is beneficial.

In some circumstances, typically regarding coastal properties, the fee management company may be able to offer the insurer a balanced portfolio, and offset the risk of a one-off coastal property with multiple inland properties.

Finally, while it doesn't offer a direct savings, management companies may be able to offer health, dental and vision insurance, as well as a 401-K plan. This benefits you because the availability of benefits may allow the management company to attract a higher quality employee. That means a better-run store and increasing profits. Typically, only larger management companies with many locations will be able to offer this benefit.

WHEN IT'S TIME TO SELL THE PROPERTY, THIS MAKING MONEY STRATEGY REALLY PAYS OFF

If you are considering selling your property, you may want to split the management fee between the ownership entity and the operations. Part of the expense then becomes a partnership expense, and part becomes an operating expense, thus increasing the Net Operating Income (NOI). If this is a practice you adopt, do so at least two years before the sale so it does not look like a forced attempt to increase the

SECTION TWO: EXPENSES - MANAGEMENT FEES

NOI. You may be able to legitimately pay the management company 4 percent for the operations on site, and 2 percent for performing duties on behalf of the ownership, such as paying the bills and preparing financial reports.

Be advised that many buyers will underwrite the project with a 6 percent fee regardless of what you are paying, since that is the industry standard. In this case, you will lose the advantage of a fee split. However, there are many less sophisticated buyers in the marketplace that do not use professionals to conduct the due diligence and will accept the lower management fee percentage. Many brokers use this trick in preparing offering memorandums (marketing packages to sell the property) to "puff up" the NOI.

Be cautious of management contracts that have additional pass through expenses for supervision, travel, and specific project management. These expenses can raise your management costs. If you cannot negotiate to remove them, at least negotiate to have them capped. This may be a compelling reason to use a local firm that does not have the expense of needing to bring in supervision from out of town to oversee on-site management.

HOW TO SELECT A FEE MANAGEMENT COMPANY

Once you have decided you are too busy to manage the property yourself, you may be faced with the task of deciding who should do the job. You have three basic options. You could vest more power in your manager and have them take on a higher level of accountability and responsibility. You can hire a fee management company. Or you could do nothing. Making more money would dictate the first and last options as least desirable, so let's focus on choosing a fee management company.

A fee management company is typically a third party, unrelated to your ownership. For a percentage of the revenues, the company will manage the day-to-day activity in the business, including hiring, supervising, training and terminating the manager and team (whose salaries are a separate expense and not included in fee management services). Fee management companies should pay all the monthly bills and produce financial statements and monthly reports for your review, as well as an annual management, marketing and staffing plan.

This may be a difficult task, as there may be only a few firms to choose from that operate in your area. There may be no firms that have self-storage experience, or the ones that do, may not have the attention to excellence that you want in your store. These scenarios could force you into the open market for a fee management solution.

If you find yourself in this position, you will be looking at a handful of firms that offer nationwide fee management services, such as Executive Self Storage Associates, or a regional player such as PDQ Management Solutions. There are some firms that limit themselves to certain states, like Self Storage Advisors from Texas. No matter which way you look, there are lots of questions. So read on for some checklists that will help you determine how best to choose a fee management company.

A LAUNDRY LIST OF POSSIBILITIES

You've got plenty of options in the realm of management companies. Indeed, the choices can be dizzying. Here is a list of questions that will help you narrow down your options:

- Should I hire someone local like PDQ Management Solutions?
- Should I hire a large national firm like Executive Self Storage Management?
- Do I contact the industry "icons?"
- Do I give preference to a local based provider?
- Are the regional firms the best of both local and national providers?
- Should I be concerned if they manage my competitor?
- How are they going to staff my store for day-to-day operations and emergencies?
- How often should the management company visit my store?

- How should I pay them?
- What are acceptable pass through expenses?
- How do I keep the management company motivated?
- How do I get preferential treatment?
- How do I hire them?
- How do I fire them?
- What should I look for in a management contract or agreement?
- What software do they use?
- Do they use combined advertising for savings?
- How do they view ancillary sales?
- Do they promote truck rentals?
- Do they prefer truck rental agency agreements or proprietary trucks? What is their experience with each, and how have they chosen to provide one or the other? Do they offer both scenarios?
- Do they want you to own or lease those trucks?
- How often do they audit the store? What is their reaction to external audits? Fear or confidence? How often do they audit the manager? Do they use internal or external resources for auditing? How thorough is the audit? What do they do with the results?

SECTION TWO: EXPENSES - MANAGEMENT FEES

- If they do audit, do they use an outside firm? Whom do they use? How much does it cost? How do they handle the information gained? Make sure that you contractually get a copy of any audits performed, both internal and external. These should be a part of your reporting requirements.
- How many owners have they fired? Why?
- What are their criteria for staff selection?
- How do they screen new-hires?
- How do they train new-hires?
- What economy of scale efficiencies do they bring to the table?
- How long have they been in business? How many clients do they have now? How many clients have they had in total? How many stores do they manage now? How many stores have they managed in total?
- How many layers of management do they have?
- How are they staffed?
- Are they well organized? Efficient?
- What kind of insurance do they carry?
- Why would they not want to manage my store?
- What other properties do they manage in my market?

- What is their vision for your store?
- What is their vision for the industry?
- How are they going to indemnify you in the event of negligence?
- What kind of professional liability insurance do they carry? Who is the carrier, and how much coverage do they have? Make certain that the individual and aggregate coverage is sufficient.
- How much coverage do they carry to insure against employee theft? What kind of claims history does the management company have, and how have the situations been handled? Did a loss result in litigation?
- When will they start?
- Do they have a transition plan?
- Are they going to keep your current staff?
- What are they going to need from me?

There are many other important questions that you should expect answers to when selecting a management company, which would include:

- What reports will I receive and on what frequency?
- Who do I communicate with regarding report data?

SECTION TWO: EXPENSES - MANAGEMENT FEES

- Who will answer day-to-day management questions?
- When and will I receive the annual budget?
- Will it offer a comparison to last year's performance?
- When and will I receive an annual marketing plan for the next year? A management plan?
- Does the image of the management company blend well with your image?
- How do the personalities of the management company owner, supervisors and staff blend with your personality?
- What is their preferred communication channel? – If the management company is e-mail centered and you do not have an e-mail account, trouble is abound. If you expect in-person handholding and the management company is not thinking the same way...trouble!
- Are they specialists in repositioning? startups? expansion sites? urban locations? suburban locations? in remote locations?
- How do they handle conflicts of interest?
- If you are a Christ-centered business, are they?

Once you have selected a few fee management companies for further consideration, have them prepare a proposal and a contract. Next, have a representative from the management company walk the store with you and explain to them what they need to know about any unique aspects of your facility. Take the time to review your financial statements with them — where you are and where you'd like to go — as well as your on-site reports. The management company should also invite you to their offices to meet their staff and better understand their organization. Be sure to get references, including a list of names and phone numbers of the last three contract terminations. You want to hear the glowing reports as well as anything that could cause you to shy away from a particular management company.

Chapter Six

SALARIES, PAYROLL & EMPLOYEES

SAVING THROUGH EMPLOYEE TRAINING

What would you say if we told you the money you spend training staff is where you will possibly see your greatest return on investment in self-storage? Well, that's what we're telling you. The paybacks are, in most cases, immeasurable because the benefits spread out to so many different aspects of the facility. A confident employee is a strong performer, so training your staff can be the key to unlocking new realms of money-making possibilities in self-storage.

In this section, we'll discuss how to set the stage for a lifetime of learning, how to get employee training off on the right foot, the various types of training styles you can choose from, the importance of specialty training, and a look at the benefits of vendor training and Internet-based training.

SETTING THE STAGE FOR A LIFETIME OF LEARNING

Your commitment to training an employee should come during the interview process. Today's employees want to learn and grow, and assuring them they will have those opportunities will help you retain the best and brightest managers. It will also set the tone for your expectations of the employee to commit to a lifetime of learning. Of course, different stages of training are appropriate for different stages of your staff's career. What's more, training may take on different forms at different times in the employee's tenure with your facility. But the concept of training, ongoing mentoring, continued education and progressive learning should be an integral part of the job description.

Granted, training and a commitment to developing an employee is always a risk. You never know how long a manager will stay on board and if he'll take his newfound skills to your competitor's facility for a higher wage. But it's a risk you must take if you want to maximize your money-making possibilities. Knowing you are interested in an employee's career development can be as motivating, if not more so, than a bonus or a pat on the back. And if you implement a culture of learning and training, then you can likewise expect your management and staff to take some responsibility for their own personal growth.

Yes, training is a two-way street. Just as the owner/operator is compelled to offer and pay for the manager's education and training – and the time it pulls him or her away from daily duties – the employee must be equally committed to devoting himself or herself to learn new information, techniques and technologies that will improve the store's process, profits and operations.

How do you know your employee is worth the resources you could spend on additional training? The answer is clear: When you see that they are willing to commit time, energy and financial resources to their own education or self-improvement. To be sure, you as an owner must see the value in an employee who is willing to attend state association-sponsored meetings and classes, or enroll in community college courses or vocational training at their own expense. The height of personal self-improvement training is the manager who invests in training from business icons and personal development trainers like Brian Tracy, Zig Zigler and Donald Trump.

TRAINING: GETTING OFF ON THE RIGHT FOOT

Training begins on the first day of employment. That may or may not be the first work day at the store. You may want to conduct orientation courses with the new employee to help them get familiar with the store policies and procedures. That way, the employee can get off to a running start. Or you may decide to have the employee dive into on-the-job training. You could also put the employee into a classroom setting or an observation mode, watching other employees or an outgoing manager do his daily routine.

Whatever form of training you choose, keep in mind than the trainer may very well be more important to the success of the program than the program itself. Never hire a trainer who isn't at the top of their field, with the best possible attitude and the most effective presentation style for your culture. If the trainer isn't passionate about training, then he or she could do more harm than good.

Far too often, self-storage operators leave the ever so important task of training to an outgoing employee who has lost his zeal for the company or the industry. If an outgoing manager is leaving because they are unmotivated, have poor attention to detail or insufficient skill sets to maintain or grow the business, then why would you want to let that person influence your fresh blood? By the same token, if you are terminating an employee because of incompetence, negligence

SECTION TWO: EXPENSES- SALARIES, PAYROLL & EMPLOYEES

or a poor attitude, why would you allow them on their way out the door to infect your new recruit? This is absolutely a disaster in the making.

SELF-STORAGE BOOT CAMP

As we mentioned, you may want to send your employee to a training center or hire a management company to begin training before the team member ever sets foot inside the store. These outside training engagements can prepare an employee to meet the rigorous demands of operating a self-storage store. The trainer should be given the ability to fully evaluate the employee's potential. After the training and the subsequent evaluation, it's up to the owner to make a potentially difficult decision of discharging the employee because they are not properly equipped or motivated to actually work in the store.

Unfortunately, too few owners terminate a mismatched manager before they start working in the store. Quite frankly, it takes a gutsy, savvy operator to make the decision to scrap the time and money invested in recruiting, hiring and training the employee only to turn around and repeat the process with no guarantees that the next candidate will be any better qualified than the last. It's up to you to decide what type of compensation the short-term employee deserves. If they left another position to work with your company and you don't plan to continue employing them, it could be a disaster for them. That's why it's such a difficult decision. But if you are sure it's not going to work out, it's still the best move for all involved.

In most cases, an opportunity does not exist for training before it is time to report to the store for active duty. Certainly it would be a rare and blessed occasion for training to occur before this day. Reality dictates, however, that many times an employee may be reporting for his first day of work after his or her predecessor has already moved on. This is perhaps the most difficult situation as there will be no opportunity for an outgoing staff member to train, mentor, observe and coach the incoming employee. Of course, the best of situations is that the employee who is leaving is doing so because you have promoted them based on their personal demonstration of excellence, competency and fantastic attitude.

ON-THE-JOB TRAINING TASKS

Turning back to our discussion of on-the-job training, this should commence with an overview of the tasks that are most important to the day-to-day operations of the business. Once the new recruit understands the basic skills required to operate the facility, then you can turn your training attention to equally important but less often used duties and practice. Here is a brief hierarchy of on-the-job training tasks:

COMPUTER SKILLS

- Take a payment.
- Move in a new customer.
- Transfer a customer from one unit to another.
- Generate an invoice for merchandise or services sold.

PEOPLE SKILLS

- Understanding the proper method for answering the phone.
- Selling the features and benefits.
- Creating a consumer desire to rent at this store.
- Meeting the needs of the client.
- Demonstrating the features of the store and the amenities.
- Solving the clients' storage related problems.
- Establishing a rapport and common ground with the prospect.
- Closing the sale.
- Understanding emergency procedures to handle situations such as fire, theft and personal injury.

STORE SKILLS

- Performing routine daily maintenance duties.
- Cleaning, cleaning and more cleaning.
- Understanding how to get things done that are outside of their personal realm of responsibility, such as getting a roof leak repaired or a light bull replaced in the sign.

While these tasks are not all encompassing, they serve as a good place to start. You as an owner/operator should build your list accordingly. When you are in the recruiting and hiring process, knowing that these are the primary functions of the position, you should make sure that the candidate is willing and able to perform all the primary tasks.

WHEN YOU HIRE FROM THE COMPETITION

That brings up our next point: hiring from a competitor. Whether that facility is across town or across the country, it's possible that your next candidate may have worked elsewhere in the industry before deciding to join your company. If the candidate has industry experience, that could be a boon. But it's not necessarily a "win-win" from an employee training perspective. We have all heard that it is hard to "teach an

SECTION TWO: EXPENSES- SALARIES, PAYROLL & EMPLOYEES

old dog new tricks." Industry experienced employees can bring with them a multitude of bad habits more easily than an equal number of new and better ideas. Be sure to make hiring decisions based on the self-storage veteran's receptivity and ability to learn new tricks, so to speak. After all, the industry is evolving on the technology and marketing fronts, among others, and there is much to learn as we continue to mature.

A self-storage management veteran who comes to the interview table with a chip on his shoulder or a know-it-all attitude is most likely not going to be open to coaching and learning. Sure, hiring someone with experience can reduce the time and effort needed to train the manager on the foundations of managing a self-storage facility. They may even offer up helpful hints and suggestions for operating the store that they have learned through trial and error at other facilities. But if they aren't open to continued learning, you may not be happy in the end.

Here's a tip: If you are considering hiring a manager or other employee from a competing facility, consider observing the employee at his current job to see if he displays a passion and competency for his work. This will help you get familiar with some of the potential candidate's habits, routines and regiments. If you don't take the time to do this, but just seek rather to woo the candidate away blindly, then you may be sorry in the end. You are starting behind the curve. You don't know the candidate's true strengths and weaknesses in practice, so you don't know how to best help them or if it's even worth trying. Consider having a mystery shopping service conduct both an in-person and telephone shop.

That brings us to a primary danger of hiring an employee who is working for a competitor: they could bring their bad habits with them to your facility. Quite frankly, you need to assess the REAL reason why they are willing to leave their current employer. Or, if they were recently terminated, you need to find out why. There may be a number of legitimate reasons for either scenario. Perhaps the store they are leaving has a small budget for salaries and the manager needs to earn a better living. Perhaps the store does not offer ongoing training opportunities and it has frustrated the employee. Maybe you are offering training and benefits, like insurance and 401(k) plans, profit sharing and bonuses, better hours and working conditions and preferred living accommodations. Or, on the flip side, perhaps the employee was getting all that and more and still couldn't cut muster. You'd be better off knowing and avoiding the headache.

SECTION TWO: EXPENSES- SALARIES, PAYROLL & EMPLOYEES

EXECUTING THE ONGOING TRAINING PROGRAM

Once the initial training has commenced and the employee understands and properly executes the basic skill sets of self-storage management, it is time to devote resources to developing superior operations skills. Remember, a new employee can bring a fresh perspective to operations. They may offer valuable suggestions about how to improve processes. In other words, they may bring change to the table. Of course, humans have a natural tendency to resist suggestions and changes in the first place, and more so, when they come from someone who has recently joined the organization. However, we must recognize the benefit of new and innovative ideas and appreciate the long-term contribution that even a small change could make.

The ongoing training program may include performing day-to-day tasks such as staying up-to-date with the latest versions of software applications. Software changes may not only require training on how to practically use the new application, but may also demand skill to convert existing databases to the new application. Software training should almost always rely on a tutorial mode to allow employees to get familiar with job functions before executing them in a live setting. The ability to measure proficiency and perform repetitive tasks, prior to using them to serve a guest or execute another management task, is critical to the employee's confidence.

Additional training may also be required when new products and services are introduced into the retail area of the property. The bottom line is this: No new program should be introduced without adequate training, so that the employees are both competent and confident. These two attributes will greatly enhance the ability of the employee to sell the new services and/or products with the desired results.

Consider implementing an annual training schedule with tasks outlined on a month-by-month basis. An older employee may want to discuss this schedule during his or her annual review and suggest ways to maximize their strengths and minimize the weaknesses. When you determine that improvement is needed in an area, resources should be allocated to offer training, personal development, education and growth in the challenging areas. You can find training programs through *Inside Self Storage* magazine or state self-storage associations. You'll find tradeshows, seminars and other educational opportunities in abundance, and you can schedule and budget for training for your employees.

Beyond management, savvy owners also seek to improve the sales skills of other front-line employees. That includes individuals who come in contact with the general public. Anyone who deals with your tenants – and potential tenants – should have sharp customer service and sales skills. That may mean sending those employees to customer service and sales improvement seminars. These seminars don't necessarily need to be self-storage industry specific. Customer service and sales skills translate to any industry.

SEEKING SPECIALTY TRAINING

You may also want to seek specialty training in one or more emerging areas. One of the fastest growing demographics in the United States, for example, is the Hispanic population. The percentage of bilingual self-storage employees is relatively small compared to the universe of total industry employed staff members.

If the demographic composition of your market indicates that the Hispanic population is anywhere near 25 percent or greater of the total population, then there is a tremendous opportunity in marketing to this group. If you hope to penetrate the opportunities this group represents, it's important that your salesperson is truly bilingual, or at least proficient enough to communicate clearly with a Spanish-only speaking tenant. Spanish-speaking customers appreciate the effort to reach out to them in their native tongue.

Owners who are serious about increasing occupancy and revenues will find value in having bilingual team members. You may be able to hire employees that are bilingual but more often than not, this skill set demands someone who either speaks Spanish as their mother tongue or who has learned through travels or education. Owners should seriously consider paying for or reimbursing the expenses for an employee to learn a second language, and such an accomplishment would be meritorious of a large bonus.

While it is possible to use software applications to teach oneself Spanish, it demands motivation, self-discipline and perseverance to complete an online or audio-based program. Your employees may have greater success with a community college course that offers Spanish courses. In either case, an employee who is willing to spend the time – paid or unpaid – to learn a second language is a tremendous asset to any organization.

TRADE SHOWS, SEMINARS AND THE INTERNET

At certain times during the year, and at trade shows, vendors hold seminars or user groups that educate their customer base on how to use and/or service and maintain their products. This includes software applications and how to use the functions of an update recently deployed – or one that will be released in the near future. It's always a good idea for staff members to get training ahead of the newly released version of the product.

At times, door manufacturers will also hold training seminars on how to maintain rollup doors. This training typically includes the use of devices for adjusting tension of the door, which is usually the most common problem

SECTION TWO: EXPENSES- SALARIES, PAYROLL & EMPLOYEES

you'll encounter. Not all door tensioning devices are easy to use, and there may be some safety issues inherent with an inexperienced individual who attempts to perform tension maintenance on a door. There are typically some very basic safety precautions that, once learned, greatly reduce the risk of injury in maintaining doors.

Not all training needs to be completed in a person-to-person environment. There are many computer-based education programs available and some even target the self-storage industry specifically. Our friends and colleagues Jim Chiswell and Mel Holsinger created the Self Storage Education Network to provide computer-based education for the self-storage industry. They have many topics of interest that are quite informative and are very inexpensive. Other resources to the self-storage industry, such as Virgo Publishing, the publishers of *Inside Self Storage* magazine, are also launching low-cost industry-specific educational programs.

It is difficult to quantify the return on investment in training. The benefits come back to the owner in so many different ways. Increased productivity, increased sales, and an added tool in the recruiting process are just a few of the salient benefits to investing in employee training. Perhaps the greatest benefit of all can be found in the employee who has had the benefit of training, has increased confidence, and comes to work with a much better attitude that can be quite contagious!

Remember this: Owners who invest in training employees are actually investing in themselves.

Indeed, training plays a vital role in making more money in self-storage.

PAYROLL & BURDEN: A SENSITIVE MATTER

The "payroll and burden" expense category is perhaps the most sensitive to a cost-benefit relationship. By paying higher salaries or offering extraordinary benefits or bonuses, you may be able to recruit a higher quality manager. A higher quality manager can make you more money in the long run.

What we're saying here is this: Saving money on salaries by paying less may not be the best strategy. Consider the table below. It demonstrates a hypothetical situation in which the owner paid 10 percent above typical salary levels for the most competent manager. That manager, as you might suspect, better managed the property by increasing revenues in the order of 3 percent and reducing expenses 2 percent. In the example salary table, you can see how dramatic that impact is on the bottom line.

SECTION TWO: EXPENSES- SALARIES, PAYROLL & EMPLOYEES

MINIMUM SALARY		HIGHER SALARY	INCREASED PERFORMANCE
$ 35,000.00	**Base**	$ 46,000.00	$ 46,000.00
$ 3,500.00	**Bonus**	$ 4,600.00	$ 6,900.00
$ 5,775.00	**Benefits & Burden**	$ 7,590.00	$ 7,935.00
$ 44,275.00		$ 58,190.00	$ 60,835.00
$ 800,000.00	**Income**	$ 800,000.00	$ 824,000.00
$ 304,000.00	**Expenses**	$ 317,915.00	$ 314,148.00
$ 496,000.00	**NOI**	$ 482,085.00	$ 509,851.20
$ 6,613,333.33	**7.5% Cap Value**	$ 6,427,800.00	$ 6,798,016.00
$ 0.00		$(185,533.33)	$ 184,682.67

Example Salary Table

If the manager or an employee is performing duties of a fee management company, as is typical in owner-operated stores, part of the on-site salary can be allocated to the partnership. That portion of the salary will fall outside of the expenses for store operations and thus increase NOI. The cost of that employee time (and the commensurate payroll burden) is paid from the ownership entity and not from store operations. An example would be, for time spent meeting with Yellow Page directory representatives in the design and placement of the ad, or if the employee handles matters on behalf of the partnership, such as paying bills, or any task that would normally be handled by a fee management company.

SHOULD YOU USE A PEO?
(Information courtesy of StaffMarket.com)

Many self-storage operators are considering the use of Professional Employment Organizations (PEO), more popularly known as employee leasing. This is a function of many management companies that may use a PEO or act as an ASO (Administrative Service Organization). The former truly manages the entire employee-employer relationship, where the ASO tends to be more of a payroll processing service.

The driving force for justifying a PEO is liability reduction. The employer may give up some control over labor quality (which is also an issue in the fee management/ASO relationship) but the intended benefit of protection and reduced liabilities may be worth the trade off in some cases. There are some simple tasks for a PEO, such as providing you with required state and federal posters, or supplying manuals with safety procedures customized to self-storage operations, or granting access to a library and educational videos on safety issues.

The more important services a PEO provides, though, are found in day-to-day operations, such as safety training for management and employees and arranging on-site inspections. Frequent on-site inspections can prevent costly

SECTION TWO: EXPENSES- SALARIES, PAYROLL & EMPLOYEES

OSHA fines, as well as fines from other government agencies, while reducing injury risk. If a claim does occur, the PEO can manage it to ensure injured employees are given the best care possible and maintain direct contact with claims insurance adjusters to expedite the return to work process.

A PEO can also provide employee manuals and handbooks, which can limit your liabilities as you simultaneously institute programs, policies and procedures. Examples include implementation of a "Light Duty" policy to minimize workers compensation claim costs, or use of progressive disciplinary measures to avoid unemployment insurance claims, which can ultimately pay for themselves through defeat of increased premiums. PEOs will often represent themselves, and ultimately the self-storage owner, in unemployment and workers compensation cases (as well as monitoring the experience modifier).

EMPLOYEES VERSUS INDEPENDENT CONTRACTORS
(Information courtesy of StaffMarket.com)

Some self-storage operators have employed PEOs to create a buffer between the employment contract they have and the desire to maintain an independent contractor relationship with the manager. This is a very risky strategy, as the consequences of losing a case are far greater than the benefits derived by "flying under the radar," under the shield of the "customary industry practice" language of the IRS.

Let's face it; if the manager must be in the office during office hours, you are setting a precedent that you are controlling their hours. This is typically prima-fascia evidence that an employee-employer relationship exits. Next comes the requirement that the manager follow certain policies and procedures, requiring training from the employer. This knocks out the independent job production and protection afforded to contractors. The requirement that all the services be performed in a location to be dictated by the employer, further exacerbates the issue. Since the employee may not set their own hours and location of the job, they often do not meet the independent contractor definition.

EXEMPT VERSUS NON-EXEMPT OVERTIME CLASSIFICATIONS

Another major controversy for self-storage owners is in the payment of wages. Many operators have chosen to require managers to work more than 40 hours a week without overtime pay. They do this under the definition of an "exempt" employee to avoid paying overtime. Once again, there is debate as to whether or not the manager qualifies for "exempt" status. The most commonly accepted self-storage definition is for "Administrative Exemptions," as defined by the Department of

SECTION TWO: EXPENSES- SALARIES, PAYROLL & EMPLOYEES

Labor. To qualify for the administrative employee exemption, all of the following tests must be passed:

- The employee must be compensated on a salary or fee basis (as defined in the regulations) at a rate not less than $455 per week;
- The employee's primary duty must be the performance of office or non-manual work directly related to the management or general business operations of the employer or the employer's customers; and
- The employee's primary duty includes the exercise of discretion and independent judgment with respect to matters of significance.

The job descriptions for executive, professional, outside sales, computer technician and highly compensated employees meet the definition less easily than if classified as an administrative employee. If you have doubts, www.paq.com offers a questionnaire that can be completed, and for a nominal fee, the position will be matched against the Fair Labor Standards Act criteria for an informal ruling.

Owner beware: The employee's exempt status may be jeopardized if you require the employee to deduct salary for partial days off, or, again, if you require the employee to work certain, set hours. It is always better to focus on the requirements of the work, instead of scheduling specific hours. As an example, instead of a job requirement that states the employee still work from 8:00 a.m. to 5:00 p.m. from Monday through Friday, simply state the primary job function: to assist customers in the rental and use of the self-storage property, and to be available during the hours that customers visit the property[2]. If the employer deducts wages from an exempt employee's pay for time missed (other than under very specific, extraordinary circumstances), the deduction may be considered an attempt to regulate pay based on an hourly basis, and therefore may create a non-exempt employee status.

Chapter Seven

TAXES

SAVING ON YOUR TAXES

This goes without saying, but we're not accountants. We're not tax attorneys either. But that certainly does not prohibit us from suggesting some tried and true strategies for saving money in self-storage by reducing your tax bill. Much like insurance expenses, reducing property and income taxes falls within the expertise realm of legal and accounting professionals. So be sure to vet this information with your tax professionals to see how it fits into your specific circumstances.

With those "disclaimers" in mind, this chapter will give you some practical advice on how to make more money in self-storage through tax savings. We'll also explore the options of appeals and give you some insights into why you may not want to fight the government's status quo. The bottom line is, you can save on taxes in many cases. But the money you save may not be worth the risk you take. Balance all possibilities with the advice of your counsel.

TAX SAVINGS STRATEGIES: COST SEGREGATION

There are some possible strategies to help save taxes. Cost segregation services (CSS), for example, is an IRS-approved process that reduces taxes and increases cash flow through accelerated depreciation. In fact, the CSS is the closest thing to an IRS windfall that most property owners will ever enjoy.

On average, a real estate owner can expect an increase in the internal rate of return and cash on cash return by 100 to 350 basis points, respectively. In most cases, an average of 20 to 30 percent of project-related costs are reclassified into shorter-lived categories. From a purchase price perspective, we have seen as much as 2 percent of the purchase price come back to the taxpayer in the form of CSS benefits. In fact, the additional cash flow benefits that the CSS provides are so outstanding that the IRS has developed a special audit technique to assist in reviewing them. It is imperative, therefore, that the taxpayer maximize CSS benefits without compromising their position with the IRS.

One way to improve the results and the reliability of the CSS is through the use of a Property Condition Assessment (PCA). The PCA is a building inspection primarily governed by American Society of Testing Materials (ASTM) standard E2018-01. In 2005 alone, there was an estimated 50,000 PCAs completed nationally. Each one of these assignments, and the related work papers, were most likely completed in accordance with the ASTM standard. These PCAs can offer self-storage owners savings and security toward the baseline work of the CSS. Indeed, the PCA & CSS work hand in hand to identify a building's physical condition while uncovering accelerated depreciation opportunities.

Owners and lenders typically require a PCA prior to closing. The PCA provides a comprehensive analysis of the building systems, accrued physical deterioration and immediate remedial requirements. Often supported by the consultant's professional liability policy, the PCA provides the lender peace of mind. Better yet, the "required" PCA can now be used to increase cash flow since it is the foundation of the properly executed CSS.

Savvy real estate owners are saving costs by using the PCA to supplement the CSS. Working together helps reduce the client's overall investment in due diligence while also saving valuable time by contemporaneously conducting both evaluations. A properly completed PCA is the only document that dovetails into the CSS scope of work perfectly. To this end, some of the same inspection processes need not be duplicated in order to determine the lucrative tax savings the CSS affords. This comprehensive approach also mitigates and controls erroneous, duplicative and inappropriate costs.

While almost all property owners are familiar with the PCA, fewer are familiar with the CSS, which is designed to identify shorter-lived assets. Though the CSS is not a new concept, many real estate owners still have not explored the IRS-approved process for increasing annual after-tax cash flow through accelerated depreciation.

Here's how it works: Instead of lumping improvement costs into the total price of the facility and depreciating the sum over the standard period of 27.5 years for residential properties and 39 years for non-residential properties under the straight-line method, U.S. tax codes allow certain tangible building components and improvements, as well as a wide range of site work costs, to be depreciated over a much shorter period - 15, 7, or even 5 years. When you compare a 5-, 7- or 15-year depreciation cycle to a 27.5- or 39-year depreciation cycle, the actual near-term cash flow increases are evident.

In addition to the benefits associated with recent acquisitions, the IRS permits a taxpayer under Rev. Proc. 96-31 to complete a Change of Accounting (Form 3115) to recoup missed depreciation for assets that are being depreciated incorrectly. This automatic process does not require amended returns and can translate into a huge windfall in terms of catch-up depreciation. For portfolio assets placed in service from prior years, a PCA completed at the time of acquisition in conjunction with a current CSS adds significant value in the event the IRS challenges the physical condition of the asset at the time of the purchase.

Chapter Eight

UTILITIES

SAVING ON UTILITIES: A BIG PICTURE VIEW

Utilities may be one of the most difficult areas to control or effect savings, once an initial adjustment is made. There are some basic steps that can be taken and more dramatic steps if the project warrants. But there comes a point that you've done just about all that you can do.

However, if you haven't done all you can do, or if you aren't sure, then you should get with the program because it could mean significant savings over the long-term. Every penny counts. In this section, we'll take an in-depth look at how to make money in self-storage by saving money on energy and water without sacrificing comfort, safety or tenant satisfaction. You could save as much as 20 percent on your utility costs with a few adjustments.

CONDUCTING AN ENERGY AUDIT

Most public utility companies offer some form of an energy audit. A technician will visit your facility to conduct the audit free of charge, typically. These utility company-sponsored audits may not be as thorough or valuable as an audit by a firm you hire, but they represent a good place to start, especially if you have not yet taken energy conservation steps.

It all starts with benchmarking where you are. You want to measure your kilowatt-hours per square foot usage and your ENERGY STAR Portfolio Manager score. You can visit www.energystar.gov online and click on "Business Improvement" to access the online benchmarking tool, which is called Portfolio Manager. From there, set up a secure account and get started. You may need the help of your utility company to determine your actual usage. If your building scores below 75 points, then there is a strong possibility you can save significant dollars on your energy spending.

When you conduct an energy audit, what you'll quickly discover is that the temperature ranges for climate-controlled space are the largest culprit of waste, and therefore potentially the largest area of savings. It is not unreasonable to set temperature ranges at 80 degrees in the winter and

SECTION TWO: EXPENSES - UTILITIES

50 degrees in the summer. Most stored goods will never experience damages within these suggested ranges. If you feel it is necessary to offer more cooling or more heating, then installing programmable digital thermostats to adjust temperature levels at night to 82 degrees and 48 degrees respectively, is worth the investment. Be sure to keep thermostats in locked boxes to discourage tenants from tampering with the equipment. Control of humidity, is an all together different issue.

Another common area in which a self-storage energy audit will reveal waste is in the tenant use of doors. You will discover that self-closing doors are another factor that could breed energy savings. Guests have a tendency to prop unit doors open during move-in or move out, with little regard for energy conservation on climate-controlled units. Consistent and constant property checks help the manager to monitor and correct these money-wasting conditions. We suggest the rules and regulations clearly state your desired practices for entrances and exits to help encourage the tenant to save energy.

Lighting fixtures also produce heat and consume electricity. If lights are burning when there is no guest activity, you are wasting energy – and losing money. Most state-of-the-art self-storage stores have a certain minimal amount of constant light that remains on all the time, and the majority of the lights only come on when motion is sensored by activity in the lighted area (perhaps every third fixture remains on at all times and the other two are on motions sensors), or perhaps even some ambient light from outside illuminates the area. The rental agreement should designate the parameters for use of lighting, and certainly should prohibit tenants from removing bulbs from fixtures and replacing bulbs with screw-in receptacles inside the spaces.

Once you've completed your energy audit and addressed the low hanging fruit, you can turn your attention to a full-fledged energy management program. This program should identify your energy priorities and a strategy for ongoing energy and cost savings. Your program should be explicit with a clear plan of action and identify who is responsible for managing the plan. There are literally hundreds of energy-saving upgrade options you could make. Here are some suggestions for reducing utility expenses:

- Change static switches, particularly hallway lighting to motion sensors or timers that automatically turn off lights when buildings are empty. For safety purposes, you may want to leave a fixture "on" every 40 feet or so.
- Reduce bulb wattages. You may choose to stagger the lower wattage bulbs every few feet to maintain a certain level of brightness while also reducing overall energy expenditures.
- Routinely check to make sure tenants are not using outlets. Over the years, meat lockers,

SECTION TWO: EXPENSES · UTILITIES

freezers and even television sets have been left on in spaces, with the owner footing the bill.

- Look for fluorescent fixtures that do not fully energize the bulbs. There may be two reasons for fixture failure: either the bulbs need to be replaced or the ballasts could be faulty. There are new energy saving ballasts on the market, and bulbs that run on lower power consumption. Higher watt, single-bulb fixtures can consume less electricity than dual-bulb fixtures.
- When constructing a new facility, or even in some existing sites, raising or lowering fixtures so that they spread the most light can be an energy-saving option that allows you to use lower watt bulbs.
- Replacing incandescent bulbs with fluorescents. It may make sense to even replace some fixtures, but at minimum, consider bulb changes.
- Clean fixtures and bulbs. Keeping lights clean also allows more light to glow, and you may be able to reduce wattage in high light areas.
- Change fixtures. There are many reflective fixtures and light dispersers that can spread light more effectively.
- Consider changing solid exit doors to doors with windows when it's time to replace them. Natural light is the most inexpensive of all!

- Investigate the possibility of replacing some (maybe even all) of the driveway light packs on your buildings, keeping only those in areas not covered with pole lighting that the utility company provides (for a fee). Because many utility companies charge a fixed fee per fixture, per month, they will opt for more expensive, energy efficient bulbs and fixtures.
- Keep door closers lubricated and maintain them for proper operation. It is a fact that guests will prop open doors when moving in or out, and in climate-controlled buildings, that can send the meter whirling. Courteous managers can check on guests (particularly at move-out) and close doors behind tenants who are not actively entering or exiting.
- Use positive signage to remind guests about doors and openings. Consider "PLEASE CLOSE DOOR" versus "DO NOT LEAVE DOOR OPEN." Use lighthearted (professional) graphics; comic graphics help to ease tension but get the message across.
- Have key tags printed with "PLEASE CLOSE DOOR" to give to guests when they rent climate-controlled space.
- Design standards may not allow you to create a vestibule in high traffic areas. The clear plastic

SECTION TWO: EXPENSES · UTILITIES

strips that create a "curtain" to keep heat or cool inside can reduce costs. Use only clear curtains so that light can come through – for both energy and safety reasons.

- Check and repair insulation, particularly around doors and windows. Over time, rubber or foam insulation can become brittle or compressed and no longer offer air tight seals.
- Reduce the operating hours of lighted signage and lighted hallways. Traffic counts may be very low from the hours of midnight and 4 a.m., so reducing the percentage of time the lights burn equally reduces consumption.

BEFORE	AFTER
8:00 p.m. (dusk)	8:00 p.m. (dusk)
	12:00 a.m. (low traffic)
	5:00 a.m. (traffic increases)
6:00 a.m. (dawn)	6:00 a.m. (dawn)
10 hours	5 hours
	50% Energy Reduction!

- In the summertime, decrease A/C use; in winter, decrease heat. Just "tweaking" the temperatures a few degrees can make a big difference in consumption.

- Make sure thermostats are locked or out of the reach or vision of the guests. Many guests will take it upon themselves to manage temperatures, and forget to reset thermostats when they leave.
- Consider dual humidistat and thermostats in moist climates. These dual controllers can maximize efficiency and offer the greatest protection for stored goods.
- Eliminate instant-on electronics. Some printers, copiers, fax-machines and computers have "instant on" or "quick restore" features. These not only consume more power, they also produce more heat, causing cooling systems to run. Just put your hand outside of an electric device fan and you can feel the heat generated by these devices.
- In the winter, use incandescent lights to replace furnaces. Did you ever see an office tower or skyscraper with lots of lights on and wonder why they need all those lights at night when the offices are empty? Some "green" offices will use the heat from the lights to warm offices at night instead of having heaters provide warmth.
- Use programmable thermostats wherever possible to change tolerances during the night and non-peak periods. These thermostats can pay for themselves very quickly.

SECTION TWO: EXPENSES · UTILITIES

CHECK YOUR CURRENT ELECTRIC RATES

- Even if you were on the correct rate last year, things can and do change.
- If your operating hours change, or you add equipment or other load, your electric usage profile will change. A different rate could save money.
- Your electric provider may have added rates that are more suitable for your usage profile and could save your business money.
- Review your operation's usage pattern. A change in the way you operate can result in savings on your utility bill.

MAINTAIN YOUR HVAC SYSTEMS

HVAC equipment that is properly maintained will use less energy and enjoy a longer life. The greatest cost associated with an unscheduled HVAC breakdown may be in lost production – not in the repair cost.

- Keep indoor/outdoor coils and filters clean. Ensure that your HVAC system circulates the correct airflow.

- Lubricate. Check electrical connections and pulleys.
- Maintain correct refrigerant charge.
- Minimize duct leakage.
- Provide adequate ventilation in compliance with local applicable standards.
- Minimize HVAC runtime while facility is closed.
- Protect temperature-sensitive materials.
- Manage recovery if your facility is on a demand rate.
- Check the age of the fans/blowers. The older the motor, the more likely that it is not energy efficient. The newer HVAC units are designed to consume less power.
- Manage motors with long run times to save energy cost.
- Replace motors under 25 hp with energy efficient motors instead of rewinding them.
- Depending on the run time, buying a new energy efficient motor can pay for itself in energy savings and may last longer than the rewound motor.
- Size loads properly for the job. Oversized motors will use more energy than properly sized motors.

WATER HEATING ISSUES

- Locate water heaters for most efficient delivery.
- Insulate water heaters.
- Ensure that the heating temperature is correct based on local requirements.
- Control water heaters with timers based on actual periods when you need hot water during the day.
- Explore opportunities for heat recovery.

INDOOR LIGHTING CONSIDERATIONS

- Depending on your electric rate and hours of operation, switching from magnetically ballasted T-12 fluorescent lamps to electronically ballasted T-8 lamps may save (T-12 = 1.5" in diameter, T-8 = 1" in diameter).
- Consider LED exit lighting instead of incandescent.
- Assess lighting levels after closing and explore opportunities to reduce lighting levels in other areas of your business. It may be more than you need.

- Group re-lamping may save on labor costs when compared to spot re-lamping.
- Explore opportunities to switch to high-pressure sodium or metal halide lighting in large open storage areas.

OUTDOOR LIGHTING OPTIONS

- Make sure lighting is adequate for safety.
- Consider using sun trackers or photocells in conjunction with electronic timers on outdoor lighting.
- Evaluate converting incandescent or mercury vapor lighting to high-pressure sodium or metal halide lighting.
- Ensure adequate turn-in lighting off of the highway.

For marketing, comfort, management and safety reasons, we are not suggesting reducing lighting in the office area unless lights are truly excessive. Take, as an example, department stores. While retailers would love to reduce utility costs they know all too well the value of lighting in retail sales, particularly in display areas. Even discount retailers do not skimp on lighting. If you have ever walked into a dimly lit or dark self-storage office, you also know the benefit of good lighting. Dark offices are unprofessional, and the "homey" look has very little value.

SECTION THREE: CREATING EQUITY AND VALUE

Section Three

INTRODUCTION

We've have broken this book down into sections, chapters and topics that largely follow the most common financial reporting structures in self-storage. However, in this section of the book – the Equity section – we find the least standardization in financial reporting. Many aspects of how equity would be charted depend on the type of entity – publicly traded companies, for example, have different equity accounts than a sole proprietorship – and the financial reporting requirements of owners and lenders.

Despite the varied charts, the equity considerations are ultimately the most critical to the end game. The gains here are often "on paper" until a capital event, such as during a refinance or sale. But these impacts can be dramatic when realized.

We place heavy emphasis on capitalization rates, which simply mean for every $1,000 in increased Net Operating

Income (NOI), the value of a self-storage property increases $14,285.71.[3] It is this huge multiplying effect that demands the need for serious attention. Many readers may dismiss this because they have no intention of selling or refinancing today. However, that is a naïve thought as many have learned that life deals many choices, not all of them within our original plan. Unless you have the key to mortality, and can control your human lifespan, the sale of your self-storage property may be within the control of your heirs. Realizing the importance of decisions that affect capitalization rates becomes hugely important. So, planning for the future needs to be done with consideration of how it may affect our estate.

Most of the factors that create a change in equity are market dynamics that are beyond our control, such as interest rates and capitalization rates. Our goal in this section of the book is to equip you with specific tools to maximize your ability to create equity based on positioning yourself for the lowest cap rate. We do not offer get rich quick schemes or the easiest answer. Many of the equity building tools that help you to make money in self-storage are long-term execution strategies.

What you will find in How To Make Money In Self-Storage, *and* How To Make MORE Money In Self-Storage are solid strategies; but strategies that will require commitment. These strategies may necessitate a change in attitude, and a paradigm shift that starts with your very perception of self-storage and ends with life-changing capital event planning. For those of you who are looking for quick fixes or "band-aid" approaches to problem solving, making money in self-storage will be frustrating, particularly with regard to equity. For the committed owners who recognize self-storage as a terrific real estate ownership vehicle, you will be enriched, empowered and rewarded.

Chapter One

EQUITY AND VALUE

A BRIEF HISTORY

The typical self-storage site has changed greatly since the birth of the self-storage industry in the 1970s. You'll find many first generation facilities located at the end of a cul-de-sac, within an industrial park, and near undesirable uses such as manufacturing plants and "gentlemen's" clubs. City planners simply did not welcome self-storage into the visible parts of town – and for good reason. Plagued by images of metal buildings with orange doors, chain link fences and gravel drives, the planners promoted the NIMBY (Not In My Backyard) philosophy. That often meant customers had to trek to the outskirts of town to store their goods.

As the self-storage product matured, the facilities became more aesthetically pleasant and the location options became more visible and accessible for customers. When money from Wall Street started pouring into the industry in 1995 – and ever since then – city planners saw (and approved) a major influx of self-storage development activity in more mainstream locations. This, coupled with planners themselves using self-storage, opened the door for even more mainstream locations. In fact, self-storage began to compete with other retail and big box users for the same land. The developers created more sophisticated tools for site selection, and with abundant capital, self-storage evolved from a secondary land use to a long-term income producing asset class, which commanded locations with better traffic, visibility and access. The search for these properties took developers away from cul-de-sacs, industrial parks and other low traffic locations.

TODAY'S SELF-STORAGE MARKETS

Do you remember that Oldsmobile ad campaign with the tag line, "It's not your father's Oldsmobile anymore"? So it goes with self-storage locations. Now conveniently located next to Wal-Marts, McDonald's and banks; self-storage can better serve its largest users: residential consumers. Indeed, self-storage has come into its own. Bragging rights among developers as to who paid the most money for a site are common. Several general marketplace, architectural, and technological developments have spurred the migration of self-storage to more mainstream locations, including conversion of vacant big box stores, mixed-use projects with car washes, strip centers and offices, zoning approvals subject to design aesthetics, technological advances in treatments of metal buildings, and strict criteria from institutional investors requiring traffic counts above 20,000 cars a day.

MUNICIPALITY SELLING POINTS

Self-storage is enjoying "higher" zoning classifications, but that doesn't mean it's always an easy sell to municipalities. There are, however, some key selling points that will often turn the heads of municipality authorities if presented appropriately. Self-storage, for example, has a low impact on city services, such as schools, sewers, water and electricity. Self-storage is also a low traffic generator. Self-storage can be a more attractive neighbor with buffered exposure to doors and driveways and minimal parking requirements. Since modern self-storage facilities pride themselves on security and lighting, this adds more security to the area overall. Need more selling points? Well, self-storage is quiet during non-peak hours and retail offices offer sales tax-generating retail sales of moving supplies and boxes. You can probably think of additional selling points, or speak with your architects and general contractor for some ideas.

WHERE DO WE GO FROM HERE?

That's a good question. Truthfully, the possibilities are quite endless. We are encouraged by developers seeking higher quality sites. While this may create some additional barriers to entry, it also acts as a "thinning" process, washing out the faint-hearted and creating more opportunities for developers who have a higher level of commitment to the business.

Increasing higher use criteria also fosters creativity in site selection. It increases the desirability of conversion sites, for example, and opens the prospects of multiple locations for the same store. What do we mean? If you can only get small parcels of land on the main traffic arterial, you could supplement your square footage with a satellite location located on a larger, off-the-beaten path site.

The higher use standards may also create opportunities to develop brownfield sites where environmental issues make the site less desirable for other uses, yet satisfactory for self-storage. And topographically-challenged sites may lend themselves to the double-loaded building (a building with ground level access to all floors in a two-story building). Again, it's undesirable for many uses, yet perfect for self-storage.

If you are not a self-storage expert, it may behoove you to seek good counsel. A consultant focused on self-storage can offer some great ideas you may not otherwise think of. But here's a few more to get your imagination going: How about co-location, or mixed-use, sites? How about vertical sites above strip center development? Surplus inventory sites? Some terrific plans have been birthed from creative discussions about challenging markets and sites.

GET PREPARED FOR THE FUTURE TODAY

Since the higher use sites require a higher level of diligence in selection, and given the obvious impact on the economics of the transaction, developers may want to focus on strong financial analysis. Make certain the return on investment is in the mid-teens at minimum. It will require a higher degree of cost and revenue forecasting to determine if the increased costs can make a project profitable, but it's more than worth it in the end. If you want to make more money with self-storage, you need to have a clear picture of what you are getting into.

Another aspect of being prepared is dealing with municipalities. Preparation could make or break a deal, so go to the presentation with well-prepared colored site plans and strong renderings. Ideally, you can find a graphic design firm to translate the drawings into photographs. We assure you, these renderings are a strategic part of your presentation. There's nothing like helping city officials see for themselves what you have envisioned. It's also a strong tool when presenting your vision to potential investors.

Whatever you do, be sure to qualify the site, quantify your investment and create value through innovative thinking and planning. Construct a high quality building with market-appropriate amenities, understand the impact of the site's use and, once again, be fully prepared for investor and municipality presentations. Both can make or break a project. Above all, have fun and make money!

THE CHANGING FACE OF STORAGE

Evolution. Improvement. Progress. Call it what you want, but it is all change. Self-storage is certainly not immune to change. As a matter of fact, the self-storage business industry has changed so dramatically in the past few decades that its roots are hardly recognizable. Whether you are just dipping your toe in the self-storage waters, you are a student of self-storage history, or are an old veteran who remembers the 'good old days,' tracking the evolution of the industry offers keen insights into how to make more money in self-storage today. Indeed, we can learn plenty of lessons from the mistakes of the past as we head to more profitable futures. We can also learn some lessons from the changes the first generation self-storage property owners are making to stay in the game.

LAND BANKING & SELF-STORAGE

Many of the industry's first self-storage projects were created as a temporary use for land. In the 1970s, development occurred where owners contemplated uses such as hotels, banks, and retail (in the right locations). So what happened to these plans? C-A-S-H! Not small amounts, but boatloads of it. Many first generation 1970 vintage self-storage properties still operate today at profit levels so great that it is hard to justify replacing the use.

Very few of the developments were closed because of failure or lack of profit. If the land use changed, it was typically because the new use was willing to greatly overpay for the asset. We're reminded of Sam, who sold an older self-storage property in Las Vegas. What sits there now, you ask? A huge casino that was willing to pay a pretty penny. Sam took the profits and built another self-storage property just a few miles away. Sam is not the only lucky duck. We've seen developers of Wal-Marts, malls, auto dealerships and others buy up self-storage sites and build their own empires. The self-storage pioneers laughed all the way to the bank.

FIRST GENERATION LESSONS LEARNED

For those first generation stores that didn't sell out, however, many of the properties are not faring too well today in terms of appearance and condition. That's because these early 'land bank' stores used inferior materials by today's standards and design, such as screw-down roofs, chain link fences, no gutters, gravel driveways, sheetrock walls, wood doors, frame-stucco construction, wood truss roofs... you get the picture. Those properties put a bit of a 'blight' on the industry's reputation as they grew older. Some store owners upgraded. Others are still in bad shape.

But there is an important lesson we can take away from this: build for the long-haul. When the industry was birthed, many couldn't see this far ahead. But today's developers see well into the future and build third generation facilities to last. Today's developers use aluma-shield panels, stronger partition and door materials, and longer lasting paints and finishes. Modern facilities use diamond plate corners and cart rails and corrugated metal office exteriors dressed with architectural treatments. The finest facilities today have replaced low-cost materials with durable, aesthetically pleasing materials – and land bank sites are no longer the target. Of course, municipalities have driven some of these changes. But developers striving to reduce operating and maintenance costs, while also building attractive facilities that win new customers, are driving most of these changes.

COSMETIC SURGERY? FACELIFT OR COLLAGEN INJECTION?

If you have an older facility, never fear. You can still increase the value of your property and make more money in self-storage – and it doesn't have to cost you a fortune. Roofs can be replaced or roofed over (the latter is a better option).

SECTION THREE: CREATING EQUITY AND VALUE

What about rusted purlins? And how do you repair rusted corrugated metal exteriors? A new skin is an option, but not a good one. There may be some opportunities to vacate a building and rebuild or totally renovate, but the risks and cash flow disruption can be devastating. Still, where there is a will, there is a way. Don't despair. Act now before the property declines any further and start adding new value today. The dividends are rewarding.

> **Before we tell you what to do, let us tell you what not to do:** Don't involve the customer. Consider that many tenants pay their monthly storage bill with the intention of vacating after a few months. Of course, they often stay for many more months – or even years – because life is busy and they don't get around to moving out. So they keep paying you. That could change if you start doing major renovations that require the tenant to move his goods. Even if you move the tenant's goods for him, you'd have to get permission to make the move. This reminds the tenant that he wanted to move his goods anyway and often leads to a new vacancy. Your best bet, then, is to create value at your facility in ways that don't involve the customer. Then, when he does come back to vacate, at least he or she will be pleasantly surprised with the improvements and may recommend your facility to a friend.

WHEN PUTTING LIPSTICK ON THE PIG JUST DOESN'T CUT IT

When it comes to older properties, we can make some common assumptions. The site is typically level, but the building roots are often "tired." The property is typically in a market that has evolved to demand climate-controlled space, but does not offer this amenity. Competitors who are offering climate-controlled units are charging a premium for the luxury. We can also assume that the drives are narrow, often about 20-feet wide, and that there is a mix of small units facing the drive. How can we assume those things? This is the pattern of most first generation facilities.

The good news is we can work with this. Here's what you can do: Convert the 20-foot-wide drive into a 5-foot-wide hallway that offers new units to the mix. You'll end up with a 10-foot wide row of spaces and a 5-foot hallway. You can put on a new roof that spans both buildings, with new doors installed at the hallways. Now – and this is the good part – you can install climate-control equipment inside the roofs of the older buildings that are being covered with a new insulated roof. You can also replace your old wood doors with swing or rollup metal doors, and install hallway doors that offer windows to allow ambient light into the facility. Next, hang some light fixtures to add life to the newly created hallways.

Are you getting the picture? This is just one option that's altogether doable. It could create tremendous value for your facility, both from a revenue perspective and a capitalization

SECTION THREE: CREATING EQUITY AND VALUE

rate perspective. In the spirit of full disclosure, there are no guarantees. Just because you make improvements to your property doesn't guarantee you will be able to increase rents. As a matter of fact, astute property managers and owners were already charging top of the market rents, even with inferior product.

The exception to that rule is climate-control. You will absolutely, most definitely increase your revenues if you add climate-controlled storage where there was none. Now, we didn't say it would be a piece of cake. If you decide not to vacate the building as you undergo the climate-control conversion project, you will be forced to let market conditions dictate what you do with the existing tenants. If demand is robust, you may have to issue 30-day notices to vacate, or fight for rent increases with the existing tenant base that did not rent climate-controlled space but may now be forced to pay to stay.

One could let the building turn to climate-control by attrition, but the payback is going to be slow. If the climate-controlled section or the building in question represents more than 10 percent of your space, you will likely want to vacate the tenants rather than wait for them to move naturally (attrition). If there are many vacancies within your property, that might be a good reason to begin moving them over, so you have an inventory with a varied mix of unit sizes in the new climate-controlled section to rent. Make this process as painless and with the least impact possible on the guest.

What if you don't have thousands of dollars to add climate-control, install new doors and hang new lights? Well, you can still do something. You could borrow money from your banker and charge ahead, or you could go to the hardware store and buy some cans of paint. Of course, this is a temporary solution that does not create or support long-term value. In other words, it may win you a few new tenants, but this is not a long-term strategy for making more money in self-storage.

GLEANING THE MOST FROM YOUR FEASIBILITY STUDY

The facts and data used to determine the original decision of where to build a self-storage property can dictate the success of the store. Ultimately, the wrong location, capitalization, or market can make it nearly impossible to make more money in self-storage. The process of determining the right location – called feasibility – is the genesis of a store.

    The nature of this book assumes the feasibility decision was made long ago and you are now working with brick and mortar, not concept. So if you need a primer on how to invest with a lengthy discussion about feasibility, pick up "How to Invest in Self-Storage." You can purchase it online at HowToInvestInSelfStorage.com or Amazon.com. With all this said, it's important to your money-making ventures to recognize that the feasibility study's usefulness does not end with site selection. You'll be glad to know that you can use your findings in several ways to create greater profits. Let's take a look at how.

SECTION THREE: CREATING EQUITY AND VALUE

REVIEWING THE FEASIBILITY STUDY

First and foremost, the feasibility study should indicate your customer base (the area's demographics) for the original store. It should document the competitive environment. Reality dictates that the world is changing, and the assumptions used to build the store many years ago may not reflect current demography or market conditions. It is not at all unusual for demographic or competitive landscape changes to occur. It is likely in most major markets that competition will increase over time. So how does the old data become useful? If the original assumptions no longer apply, and the store is operated in the same manner as it was before the change in demographics, then that alone indicates the need and justification for a change in operations.

GOING BACK TO THE 1980s

As an example, let's assume the store was constructed in 1982. The industry standards in the early 1980s were dramatically different than they are today. It might have been appropriate at that time to build a 150-square-foot office attached to a 500-square-foot caretaker's quarters. Today, generation-next or state-of-the-art stores may boast 900-square-foot offices and retail sales areas to sell boxes, rent trucks and mobile storage containers, offer pack and ship services and online auction processing. The space requirement could easily absorb the apartment space and justify a full conversion of the apartment to retail space. The decision to remodel according to today's standards should be determined based on a new feasibility study to assess the return on investment for the converted space.

PRE-2003 CONSTRUCTION CONSIDERATIONS

The metrics and drivers used in pre-2003 site locations have also changed with regard to original feasibility. These older locations, which in very old stores may have included dead end streets, cul-de-sacs, industrial parks and low traffic locations, which were considered feasible at that time, would be unacceptable today. The modern location is retail-oriented and site selection for a strong self-storage location may not differ substantially from big box retail site location criteria.

If the original location chosen is highly inferior to the state-of-the-art competitor's locations, then increasing profits may take more effort. But you can still use the original feasibility study to attempt to make more money in self-storage. Specifically, the use of the original feasibility study and the marketing techniques initially deployed will create analytical tools to allow measurement of how successful the old methods of operations are compared to the current trends.

SECTION THREE: CREATING EQUITY AND VALUE

Obtaining a feasibility study is traditionally reserved for new projects. More and more, however, savvy operators are enjoying the benefit of getting up-to-date marketing data, long after the store is opened. This current information can be useful when considering store repositioning, expansion, new construction or when occupancy falls below desired levels. Hiring a reputable consultant to prepare a feasibility study is a proven way to get an objective, professional opinion about your market. Armed with that data, the consultant may be engaged to audit your store and provide keen insight with regard to turning a store around.

We have all heard that old saying "can't see the forest for the trees." Making use of a fresh, experienced mind that can evaluate your market and store without preconceived notions is a strategic approach to a difficult task.

DESIGN STANDARDS & SITE CONFIGURATIONS

Design standards and site configurations can add value to a self-storage facility. In fact, engaging a feasibility study consultant, architect, lawyer, broker and contractor on your team can make a tremendous impact on the end results. Relying on the expertise of seasoned professionals will pay dividends in the short- and long-term. Working with the industry's elite consultants may cost more than working with relative newcomers, but you may recoup long-term savings in operational costs and immediate savings in a reduction of change orders.

What's more, you are more than likely to benefit from choosing peer group professionals. There are even a few developers that require all project professionals to own at least a small stake in the self-storage facility to ensure that they keep the best interests of the facility top of mind with every decision.

In this chapter, you'll learn how decisions made in the earlier stages of a project – during concept and design – can make a radical impact on operations. We'll discuss issues like the "up versus out" debate, as well as property investment and capital considerations on the way to making more money in self-storage.

UP VERSUS OUT

One of the first decisions you'll need to make is deciding whether to build up or out. In other words, should you build a horizontal or vertical configuration for self-storage projects? This issue has caused a great debate among industry gurus, and there are clearly arguments for each option. Our job here is not to persuade you, as for sure the choice depends on various factors that could be different from site to site. Rather, our job here is to give you some basis for making the right decision for your site. That begins with understanding what drives your decision, see the Assumption and Rationale Table on the next page.

SECTION THREE: CREATING EQUITY AND VALUE

ASSUMPTION	DECISION DRIVER/RATIONALE
I own the amount of property that will support the decision I am making.	**Vestment in the property:** The site is already owned and is too small for a horizontal configuration.
Construction costs are less expensive.	**Capitalization:** Single story construction is less expensive than multi-story, and the land costs are greater than the construction costs per square foot.
I can get more footage if I go vertical.	**Economics:** Sometimes a site will be limited by a coverage requirement and the only way to build enough square footage to meet institutional grade sizing criteria is to go up.
I can only get exposure by going aerial.	**Vestment in the Property:** If the property sits below street level or behind another building or use, it may be necessary to go up several floors to get the desired visibility.
Yield limitation.	**Entitlements/Zoning:** Sometimes the municipalities are going to dictate the configuration.
Everybody else is built that way.	**Herd Mentality:** If all of the competitors are multi-story, then that must be the way to go, right?
The proven market says it will rent.	**Market Research/Feasibility:** An unbiased demand study indicates that the best design is either up or out.

Assumption and Rationale Table

The last rationale, research, may supercede all other assumptions and decisions. The practical answer is that if the market is strong enough, it will allow for multi-story. The Self-Storage Association demand study indicated that consumers still have a preference for drive-up space as compared to limited access. The last reason – when the market says it is acceptable and it is documented by an unbiased demand study – should be the only justification for this decision. If your homework supports absorption, then that is a good reason to build up or out. Any other reason has serious flaws.

INVESTMENT IN THE PROPERTY

As we mentioned in an earlier chapter, folks who already own land and have heard through the grapevine that self-storage is a good investment often charge ahead with development plans. This same group, however, also makes plenty of mistakes in the process. That's because these land owners have no idea whether or not self-storage is truly the highest and best use of the site. They only know that self-storage is a possible use. Those two views are not always congruent. While few self-storage projects actually fail – and that's by all means good news – properties that are poorly located often fail to meet the return expectations of developers and investors.

> **Here's the mistake:** Many owners will build multi-story or design a project driven by the parameters of the land they own, not because they are properly designing a project. If the site is only an acre, maybe it would be better to build something other than self-storage rather than force that use by going vertical, particularly if that is not the right market for multi-story.

SECTION THREE: CREATING EQUITY AND VALUE

Just because you only own one acre does not mean you would build vertical. Would you build a two story grocery store? Not likely. In certain circumstances, yes, but these are few and far between. Perhaps you are located behind a one-story development (existing or future), and you have heard only part of what a consultant has to say and you are looking for exposure, so you build up rather than out. Again, only a smart move if the market indicates you can rent the upstairs space. Building up, over the top of another use, is not the same as building on a parcel that has road frontage. Trying to compensate for the lack of direct visibility by going "aerial" is a mistake.

Many markets are single-story markets, dictated by the type of users and the average sized space in the market driven unit mix. Those projects with very large average unit sizes, or where the uses are largely commercial, (where more space per client is desired) are where multi-story use is less desirable. Remember that everything that goes inside a self-storage space has to be carried into the space, either on a cart or someone's back and arms! The larger the space, the more trips it takes to fill the space. The larger the stored item, the more difficult it is to load and unload through a door, through a lobby, into an elevator, through a lobby, and then down a hall into a door. What is the other option? Direct access drive up...from vehicle into the space.

At the time of publication (August 2008), there are at least two automated or roboticized self-storage projects currently in development. The robotics system is a mobile storage and self-storage hybrid which will permit drive up access to self-storage units – without cumbersome insulated roll-up doors. You may contact Coast-To-Coast Storage for more information as it is made available.

CAPITALIZATION CONSIDERATIONS

Doubtless, it costs less to build a single-story product than a multi-level product overall. However, the cost per square foot of building up should only be a fraction of the analysis. If you are building a self-storage project "on the cheap," then there are other equally significant ways that will get you into similar trouble because of under capitalization or being "cheap," such as taking an inferior location because it is less expensive, and so on. But let's stick to the issue of "up versus out."

It is not just the issue with the cost of the second story, the elevators, fire escapes, fire suppression, etc. The most devastating detriment to the project is the loss of rentable square footage due to common areas (hallways). Your feasibility study should dictate the cost differences between a single and multi-story building and offer you numbers that predict the project's ability to hit target square footage yields.

Your feasibility study should also address rental rate variances in multi-story storage to compensate for market acceptance. Many stores may have to discount the upper floor space in order to drive rentals to that space. Imagine how much less convenient it is to use a 10x10 upstairs and 150 feet down a hallway (not an uncommon design flaw) than to drive right up to the space. In case you haven't noticed, multi-story is darned inconvenient, and if you do not believe me, run a California-King sized box spring and mattress off the truck, onto a cart, into a building, up the elevator, down the hall 120 feet, off the cart and into the space. Think about it.

UNDERSTANDING THE SHEER ECONOMICS

Let's consider for a moment the loss of rentable space due to common areas. In drive-up ambient space, there is 100 percent utilization of the building. None of it is non-rentable. The moment you add a door and a hallway, the rentable efficiency of that building begins to deteriorate. In an average project, a self-contained multi-story building is going to lose 20 percent to 25 percent of the rentable space to common areas such as hallways, and oh, yes "staging areas" like vestibules and places to store carts.

Perhaps in order to meet institutional grade criteria – a real plus if you are lucid enough to consider the exit strategy – you decide you have to build "up" in order to get at least 50,000 square feet net rentable. This is perhaps an, "I have some good news and some bad news" notion. The good news is that the store meets the minimum (and I repeat minimum) requirement of 50,000 square feet net rentable required by the institutions. The bad news comes when you do not listen to the feasibility study consultant and ignore the demand factors, indicating a properly-sized project of 65,000 square feet. You decide that by building "up", you can get 200,000 square feet, and the numbers look really good. But that's only true if it rents. If the demand is for 65,000 square feet and you build 200,000 because you can, then how are you going to rent the other 135,000 square feet? What does the demand study say the absorption period will be? What is stabilized occupancy? What does the market say can be absorbed? You must listen to the answers of these and other, related questions.

ENTITLEMENTS: NOT A GOOD REASON

One of the worst factors on which to base your decision on whether to build up or out is what the municipality will allow. Some developers have decided to build out rather than up because a municipality imposed a height limitation. The decision did not make economic sense due to the cost of the land and how much had to be bought to get to institutional grade sizing.

Let's say you could buy 2.5 acres at a reasonable price, say $400,000 per acre. This will dictate (with reasonable coverage requirements) that you build vertically. However, the market is clearly a single-story (horizontal) market. In order to get 50,000 net rentable square feet of storage, you have to buy a five-acre parcel. Now the land cost skyrockets from $1 million to $2 million and the project does not "pencil." We've seen other interesting cases where the yield requirements and green space requirements created a need to build vertically. However, the market was not a vertical market, and the project has been very slow to rent, thus creating long periods of negative cash flows, dragging down returns.

AVOIDING THE HERD MENTALITY

If the head duck walks horizontal, so shall we, but we might run into a highway of cars instead of the nearest pristine lake. If you want to create a site that creates value for a project, avoid the herd mentality. There was a market in Alabama in which years of precedence said self-storage facilities should offer direct access drive up spaces. One brave soldier saw a high demand for climate-controlled storage. So he pioneered hallway access climate-controlled storage. Now, in one small market alone, there are four other similar projects.

This developer avoided the herd mentality. He went against the grain. And he created value for his project. He wasn't lucky or even betting on a hunch. Rather, this developer understood the market demand for climate-controlled space – and that the demographic data supported the use – and built the "big building" in spite of the peer group telling him "it will never rent." Now, because of the success of this pioneer, two other developers have built similar structures.

Avoiding the herd mentality is simply a matter of your appetite for risk, and your proclivity to think and invest outside of the box. If all your previous investments have been certificates of deposits, err to the side of safety with your first self-storage development. For the faint of heart or risk-adverse, go with a proven performer if the market does not answer the question.

Here is a dependable rule of thumb: People store the way they live and work. If they live in high rises or work in multi-story office buildings, they are accustomed to elevators and hall constraints. This type of consumer will not have severe objections to building up.

MARKET RESEARCH AND FEASIBILITY

Read the subtitle above once again. These are the reasons you make a decision. A decision based on these reasons will ensure a facility with value that will make you more money. In this scenario, you have done your homework to collect the data, and you have also analyzed and made an informed, educated, intelligent decision. Your decision took into consideration, issues like demand, economics, demographics, absorption, and overall market conditions. Then and only then, should you allow constraints of a site dictate your decision.

SECTION THREE: CREATING EQUITY AND VALUE

MAKING LEMONADE OUT OF LEMONS

Now, let's assume you based your decision to go vertically or horizontally on the wrong factors and you have suddenly had a rude awakening after reading this chapter. Don't fret; you can still make lemonade out of those proverbial lemons. Indeed, superb management can mitigate the wrong decision to a certain extent. Mind you, we're not talking about good management. We're not even talking about great management. We're talking about unparalleled management skills.

We discussed management companies and how to choose the right one in another chapter. For now, suffice it to say that your store manager should be strong on leadership and initiative. The manager's success will stem from hands-on involvement and commitment to the product, the project and, most importantly, the customer. If the management believes in the product and understands the use of feature-benefit consultative selling, then even a wrong decision can be made better – and with a minimum economic impact.

The "up" vs. "out" debate will continue for many years. The bottom line is that you have to let the market primarily dictate what you build, not the municipality or the costs. Always remember the "trifecta of trouble" for multi-story projects:

1. **Increased costs**
2. **Market acceptance**
3. **Net rentable square foot loss to common areas**

Multi-story self-contained buildings are a major improvement in self-storage. They tend to be cleaner, safer and easier to control pests and access. They are more prolific in their presence and afford architects a lot more room for creativity than rows of metal buildings at ground level. The problem is, sometimes, they just do not make economic sense, especially for those of you bound on making more money in self-storage.

DEALING WITH DISPOSITION

The challenge with making more money, relative to value growth or capitalization is that the money made is mostly "theoretical." In other words, unless a capital event occurs, such as a refinance or sale, the money made is on paper only. Monetizing the gain will create two specific issues. In the case of a refinance, it will create increased monthly obligations. In a sale scenario, it could cause cash flow terminations.

The most obvious and greatest advantage occurs in the refinance scenario. Since borrowed money is not taxable, and the interest is deductible, the net dollars in borrowing are typically much greater. This is amplified when the costs of a sale are considered.

The Capital Gains Analysis Table on page 178 demonstrates value creation over a 5- and 10-year period. It might be argued that the 1031 striker exchanges level the playing field, but 1031 exchanges are only a deferral of the liability, transferring the liability from one property to another. Ultimately, the proverbial piper must be paid. Arguably, the possibility exists that capital gains taxes may be reduced at final disposition, making the exchange more valuable. There are three inherent issues in executing this strategy: (1) You have to bet that the "Fed" is going to lower taxes; (2) Inflation must be in check, i.e. your dollar must grow in value; or (3) You must have an investment vehicle with greater returns than the existing asset.

WHAT ABOUT RELIEVING STRESS ON MANAGEMENT?

Some will now point out that exiting the asset relieves the stress of management. A strong argument could be made that a competent management company can mitigate the management risk. A much weaker argument is that a sale creates equity that can be placed into the next investment. Debt monies can also be invested and use of borrowed money increases return (at least on paper).

A Capital Gains Analysis highlights the increased returns, indicating a technically infinite return on equity for the new money placed. This infinite return is created because the equity placed in the second investment is done with tax-free debt (borrowed) dollars. This is where the distinction of equity and cash play an important role in return analysis. At the end of the day, however, it is all about the Benjamin's, baby, and the analysis shows that there is a *(Continued on pg. 180)*

CAPITAL GAINS ANALYSIS

SALE OF ASSET @ 5% NOI GROWTH REFI & HOLD FOR 10 YEARS AND SELL		
Original Purchase Price	$6,750,000.00	Original Purchase Price
Plus: Capital Improvements	$0.00	Plus: Capital Improvements
Less: Accumulated Depreciation	$300,000.00	Less: Accumulated Depreciation
Total Net Adjusted Basis	$6,450,000.00	Total Net Adjusted Basis
Sales Price	$11,634,962.00	Sales Price
Less: Net Adjusted Basis	$6,450,000.00	Less: Net Adjusted Basis
Less Selling Expenses	$349,048.00	Less Selling Expenses
Total Capital Gain	$4,835,914.00	Total Capital Gain
Depreciation Recapture @ 25%	$75,000.00	Depreciation Recapture @ 25%
Federal Capital Gains @ 15%	$680,387.10	Federal Capital Gains @ 15%
State Capital Gains @ 5%	$241,795.70	State Capital Gains @ 5%
Total Taxes Due	$997,182.80	Total Taxes Due
Sales Price	$11,634,962.00	Sales Price
Less: Mortgage Loan Balances	$6,218,728.00	Less: Mortgage Loan Balances
Less: Selling Expenses	$349,048.00	Less: Selling Expenses
Less Total Taxes Due	$997,182.80	Less Total Taxes Due
Ttl After-Tax $ Proceeds Yr 10 Sale	$4,070,003.20	**Ttl After-Tax $-REINVESTED**
Plus: Cash Flows	$4,367,735.67	
Refinance Proceeds	$1,249,999.75	
TOTAL CASH TO OWNER	**$9,687,738.62**	

SECTION THREE: CREATING EQUITY AND VALUE

Provided By Spectrus Real Estate Group [4]

	REINVEST ON 10% GROWTH ASSET AND SALE IN YEAR 10	
$6,750,000.00	Original Purchase Price	$2,756,667.20
$0.00	Plus: Capital Improvements	$0.00
$200,000.00	Less: Accumulated Depreciation	$300,000.00
$6,550,000.00	Total Net Adjusted Basis	$2,456,667.20
$8,333,333.00	Sales Price	$7,150,085.00
$6,550,000.00	Less: Net Adjusted Basis	$2,456,667.20
$249,999.00	Less Selling Expenses	$214,502.55
$1,533,334.00	Total Capital Gain	$4,478,915.25
$50,000.00	Depreciation Recapture @ 25%	$75,000.00
$200,000.10	Federal Capital Gains @ 15%	$626,837.29
$76,666.70	State Capital Gains @ 5%	$223,945.76
$326,666.80	Total Taxes Due	$925,783.05
$8,333,333.00	Sales Price	$7,150,085.00
$5,000,000.00	Less: Mortgage Loan Balances	$0.00
$249,999.00	Less: Selling Expenses	$214,502.55
$326,666.80	Less Total Taxes Due	$925,783.05
$2,756,667.20	**Ttl After-Tax $ Proceeds**	**$6,009,799.40**
	DIFFERENCE	**$3,677,939.22**

(Continued from pg. 177) gain of $3,677,939.22 in refinancing and holding the property, even if the replacement property grows at twice the rate as the currently owned asset.

THE KEY TO DISPOSITION

The key to disposition is a matter of timing. If there is a compelling reason to believe that a diminution value is eminent, then a sale may be a viable option. A rare investment climate exists just prior to the time of this publication (August 2008). In this unique era, self-storage operators who sell their properties are able to extract future, unrealized, hypothetical equity (also called puffing). The extraction of these unrealized gains through asset liquidation places tremendous strain on the purchasers to make more money with the asset, given their very high basis.

The Acquisition analysis table on page 181 demonstrates a time period earlier than 2006 (perhaps more indicative of normal market conditions) juxtaposed to the 2006-2007 investment environment. It should be noted that as 2008 has progressed, there are fewer properties selling at low cap rates on pro forma income. This has been evidenced by a tremendous number of price reductions, created by the "puffing" that did not sell.

PRE 2006 VERSUS POST 2006 ACQUISITION ANALYSIS

BEFORE 2006		2006 TO 2007	
TRAILING 12 MONTH NOI	$500,000	PROFORMA NOI	$750,000
Cap Rate	8.50%	Cap Rate	7.00%
Sales Price	$5,882,353	Sales Price	$10,714,286
		Difference	$4,831,933
HOW TO MAKE MORE MONEY IN SELF-STORAGE BUY			
TRAILING 12 MONTH NOI	$500,000		
Cap Rate	6.75%		
Offer Price	7,407,407		
PROFORMA NOI	$250,000		
Cap Rate	9.75%		
Offer Price	$2,564,103		
TOTAL OFFER	$9,971,510		
		Difference	$742,776

Acquisition Analysis Table

A possible scenario where timing may play a more critical role in disposition is when competitive forces impose greater burdens on properties in inferior locations. As impossible as it may seem, there are currently many buyers of self-storage in the marketplace that do not conduct thorough market research and due diligence before they acquire self-storage assets. A seller may be liquidating a self-storage property, for example, knowing a new property is in development that is controlled by an operator with a history of predatory pricing during rent up.

Disposition is the "grand finale" of self-storage ownership. All the planning, design, joys, headaches and tears end at the sale. Given this significance, disposition should be one of the most important parts of the ownership experience. There is no greater time to ensure you have made every attempt and executed every strategy to increase NOI. This is the time to remember that for each $1 you have generated in the last year, you are going to be paid $14.[5] To put it in finality...making money in self-storage ends here!

AFTERWORD

As we close this book, we'd like to leave you with these words, "If it is not measured, it is very difficult to improve." The only way to truly determine whether or not the strategies you've learned - and diligently employed – from this book are making you more money in your self-storage venture is to measure results. But you need something to measure against. That means establishing a benchmark, or baseline, of where you are right now.

Unfortunately, many owner-operators become apathetic about tracking Net Operating Income (NOI) because it may not have changed much from month to month once the facility occupancy reaches stabilization. Even a decrease in occupancy when coupled with rental rate growth could go unnoticed if the bottom line does not move. Surely, it is good news if revenues increase to cover growing expenses. But if the increased expenses are not attributable to the increase in income (such as an increase in percentage of income-based management fees), then money is left on the table, so to speak.

Before embarking on new money-making strategies,

systems or initiatives found in this book or elsewhere, it is important to look at the past to determine the strengths and weaknesses of the existing operation. Evaluating the status quo begins with reviewing historical data about your operations. Before you take large steps to boost profits, look for trails and indications that may point to problems or issues that need to be addressed in order to stabilize income and expenses. Most of the strategies in this book aim to help you take your store to the next profitability level, not to offer a quick fix for a long-term problem, systems breakdown, or other operational challenges.

More far-reaching than an increase in NOI is the capitalized value of an increase in net profits. As of February, 2008, roughly speaking, each $10,000 in NOI growth equaled $142,857.14 in value.[6] As you can see, if you keep value growth in focus, it will make money-saving and revenue-increasing efforts, even in small amounts, more meaningful. While it is true this increased value is only realized in a sale, the ratio is so impressive it is worth tracking. If you realize the importance of each NOI dollar, then it becomes more meaningful than the devaluation when NOI is reduced. It defies logic, but it is human nature to feel that we have lost money when the value decreases. We are somehow less likely to feel that we have "made" money when the value increases! That reasoning should be incentive enough to know the impact NOI has on value.

Few, if any, of these suggestions will work without the full support of ownership and all levels of management,

AFTERWORD

not only the management of people, but the management of processes. This simply means everyone in the chain of execution must have buy-in to the ideas. The weakest link in the chain will impede maximum results. Most importantly, the commitment must be fully vested at the operative level. A weakness at the store is likely to be the most devastating to achieving results. Once you have measured the success of the finest strategies you have deployed, it will be much easier to roll out others if the entire team is aware of the cause and the results. Sharing in the increase of profits is highly encouraged to achieve optimum results. What better scenario can you think of, than you and your employees making more money in self-storage by pulling in the same direction?

The implementation of ideas, concepts and strategies may require additional resources. An unmotivated management team, already burdened with critical issues or other stores or areas of operation, may not commit themselves to the process. It may be necessary to employ consultants to execute the strategies. If you need help with these strategies, contact Coast-To-Coast Storage or Self Storage Promotions. We're glad to help!

NOTES:

1. A double truck ad covers a two-page spread. That means the two-page ad is not split up between the front of one page and the back of another when the book is open, but is displayed side-by-side.

2. This is a suggestion, and the actual verbiage should be determined by a legal or employment professional.

3. Assuming a 7% capitalization rate, not unreasonable at the time of publication (06/2008)

4. http://www.spectrusgroup.com/Capital-Gains-Calculator.aspx

5. Based on January 2008 capitalization rates

6. Market Value Based on a 7% capitalization rate

CREDITS

**MAKING MONEY WITH
OUTDOOR ADVERTISING**   *Pg 19*

Provided by Tony Lockridge at www.Lockridgeoutdoor.com
Lockridge Outdoor Advertising
2091 E Murray-Holladay Road
Suite 20
Holladay, UT 84117
Phone: 801-272-2922
Fax: 800-483-1073
tony@lockridgeoutdoor.com

SHOULD YOU USE A PEO?   *Pg 120*

**EMPLOYEES VERSUS
INDEPENDENT CONTRACTORS** *Pg 121*

Provided by Jim Hamilton at www.staffmarket.com
StaffMarket Services
431 12th Street West, Suite 202
Bradenton, Florida 34205
Phone: 941-750-9450
Fax: 305-675-2872

REFERENCE

CHART OF ACCOUNTS *(Ref. page 30)*

REVENUE
Rents
Rent - Other
Rent - Climate Controlled
Rent - Past Due Collected
Rent - Mixed Use Other
Rent - Mixed Use Retail
Rent - Ordinary Storage
Rent - RV & Boat
Rent - Special
Rent - Wine Storage
    LESS COLLECTION LOSS
    LESS DISCOUNT (CONCESSIONS)
    LESS DISCOUNT (FOR PREPAY)
    LESS MISC. CREDITS
    LESS REBATES
    LESS NSF CHECKS
    LESS VACANCY

Other Income
Admin Fees
Auction Fees
Brokered Product (Commissions)
Insurance Sales (Commissions)
Late Charges
Lien Fees
NSF Fees
Other Income-Other
Security Deposits Retained
Boxes
   LESS INVENTORY COST
Locks
   LESS INVENTORY COST
Moving Supplies
   LESS INVENTORY COST
Pack & Ship Revenues
   LESS INVENTORY COST
Specialty & Other Sales
   LESS INVENTORY COST
Vending Sales
   LESS INVENTORY COST
Other Non-Revenue
Commissions
Gross Receipts
   LESS COSTS
Mileage Reimbursement

Moving Supplies
Truck Rents

EXPENSES
ADMINISTRATIVE AND OFFICE
Auction Fees
Legal
Legal Advertising
Other Collection
Computer Consulting
Computer Equipment
Computer Installation
ISP: Connection/High Speed
Other Computer
Computer Repairs
Computer Software
Computer Supplies
Computer Upgrades
Security Equipment Rental/lease
Other Security
Security Pagers & Cell Phones
Security Service
Special Security
Rent Equipment
Rent Non-owned Land or Buildings
Rent Tools
Rental Truck Fuel

Rental Truck Insurance
Rental Truck Lease Payments (On the Move, etc.)
Rental Truck Repairs
U-Haul Expenses
Rental Truck Advertising
Other Truck Rental Expenses
Answering Service
Dues
Other Office
Pagers
Permits & Licenses
Postage
Printing
Subscriptions
Supplies
Water (Bottled)
Auto Insurance
Auto Lease Payments
Employee Mileage
Fuel
Other Auto
Auto Repairs
Bank Fees
Credit Card Fees
NSF Fees
Miscellaneous and No Other Category

ADVERTISING & MARKETING
Brochures
Call Center
Cha-Chi's
Direct Marketing
E-Commerce
Other Advertising
Mailers (Val-Pak/Direct)
Supplies
TV-Radio
Web Hosting
Yellow Pages

INSURANCE
Automobile (Other than truck)
Flood
General Liability
Other Insurance
Truck - Rental
Physical Damage
Umbrella
Windstorm

MAINTENANCE AND REPAIRS
Building
Carpentry
Conveyance & Elevator

Doors, Halls, Walls
Electric
Equipment
Gate
Janitorial/Cleaning
Office (Paint/Cleaning)
Other M&R
Pest Control
Plumbing
Security & Alarms
Supplies
Tools
Trash Removal
Landscape R/R
Landscape Service
Snow Removal
Lot Sweeping

MANAGEMENT
Other Management Costs
District Management
Professional Management Fees
Marketing Consulting
Management Consulting
General Consulting
Telephone- Management Cellular

REFERENCE

SALARIES, PAYROLL & EMPLOYEE
401-K
Advertising
Agency Fees
Benefits
Bonus
Contract Labor
Education
FICA
FUTA
Insurance-Health
Insurance-Life
IRA Expense
Medicare
Other W&S
Overtime
Reimbursement
Uniforms
Salaries
Salaries-Management
Salaries-Maintenance
Salaries-Relief Management+C21
SUTA
Temporary Help
Training
Travel
Workers Comp

TAXES
Personal Property
Real Estate
Other

UTILITIES
Cable TV
Electric
Gas
Other
Septic
Sewer
Telephone-Cellular Site
Telephone-Cellular Mgmt/Owner
Telephone-Local
Telephone-Long Distance
Water

ABOUT RK KLIEBENSTEIN

RK began his self-storage career in 1985, converting incubator space to self-storage use. He then joined National Self Storage and while there was a Partner in Self Storage Mortgage Corp His self-storage financings total in excess of $200 million. After his finance career, RK joined the Amsdell Companies where RK was responsible for the acquisition and integration of more than $125 million in self-storage properties. Since that time, RK has worked and consulted on behalf of clients and employers, analyzing, acquiring, developing and integrating a wide variety of self-storage projects. During his career, RK has underwritten over three billion dollars in self-storage transactions. He estimates he has reviewed over 8,000 sites, analyzed 400 million square feet of storage space and personally seen more than 480,000 roll up doors!

RK is now the President of Coast-To-Coast Storage, offering feasibility studies, site selection, financing, management consulting, marketing and technology repositioning of older first generation facilities to compete with state-of-the-art stores. Coast-To-Coast has taken the initiative to expand the self-storage world to include mobile storage, RV/Boat Storage and Condominiums, records management and store-within-a-store profit centers. Coast-To-Coast is the world's leading self-storage consultancy firm.

In September, 2005, RK and co-author Scott Duffy released the book "How To Invest In Self Storage" through the publisher Minico. Book sales are brisk and the book is available on-line at minico.com and Amazon.com. His second and third books, "How to Make Money In Self-Storage" and "How to Make More Money In Self-Storage" are now available.

RK lives in South Florida, where he is active in his Church community, golf, boating, beach activities and nearly anything that takes him into the sunshine with his wife Lorraine.

A world-wide industry known speaker, author and expert witness, RK has experience in acquiring, developing, managing and financing self-storage properties.

ABOUT JENNIFER LECLAIRE

 Jennifer LeClaire is the founder of Self-Storage Promotions, the industry's only full-service marketing, public relations and advertising agency.

Jennifer has been serving the self-storage industry since 2001 with writing, editing, ghostwriting, public relations and graphic design services. That industry-specific knowledge, combined with her decades of media savvy, positions her to help self-storage companies promote their brands.

Jennifer has worked with Universal Studios, the NBA, the New York Times, the Associated Press, and many large and small corporations in their quest for communications excellence.

Jennifer is also president of Revelation Media Networks, Inc., an integrated marketing communications firm, and parent company of Self Storage Promotions. The Revelation Media

Networks corporate family also includes JenniferLeClaire.com. Jennifer is also co-founder of Conversion Press, an independent publisher that produced Wiley Publishing's [3]Web Analytics For Dummies" and the author of "QuestionPro for Dummies."

Jennifer is a member of the Public Relations Society of America, the American Society of Authors and Journalists and the Web Analytics Association. You can e-mail her at jennifer@selfstoragepromotions.com.

Need to declutter your marketing efforts?

SELF STORAGE PROMOTIONS

"BEYOND THE BOX STORAGE MARKETING"

Led by Jennifer LeClaire, Self Storage Promotions is the storage industry's only full-service public relations, advertising and marketing agency that exclusively serves the needs of companies like yours.

Whether you are a real estate brokerage, a storage consultant, an industry association or a self-storage facility, Self Storage Promotions has the keys you need to take your company to the next level. We accomplish this through:

- Strategic Consulting
- Public, Community & Media Relation
- Corporate Communications
- Marketing & Ad Campaigns
- Web Services
- Grand Opening Events
- Branding/Corporate Identity

For a free, 30-minute consultation on where your promotional breakdowns are occurring, call 954-454-0072 or visit www.selfstoragepromotions.com.
Experience beyond the box storage marketing.

Coast-To-Coast Storage Consulting

Your **#1** resource for self-storage consulting has solutions for self-storage developers, investors, and operators.

Feasibility Studies
- Self-Storage
- Boat and RV Storage
  (rental and condominiums)
- Mobile Storage

Other Services
- Acquisition Due Diligence
- Consulting To Increase Profits
- Brokerage
- Financing

Call us at 877-622-5508

"You can get your advice from someone who read the book or from the guy who wrote the books."

Coast-To-Coast Storage, 533 Muirfield Dr, Atlantis FL 33462
www.askrk.com email: rk@askrk.com

Coast-To-Coast Storage Consulting
Turn-Key Solutions to help YOU INCREASE PROFITS

ATTRACT COMMERCIAL CLIENTS & GAIN NEW RENTERS WITH AN IN-STORE RETAIL SHIPPING CENTER. The products, equipment and training are all included in this turn-key program – all you need is the location. This is not a franchise, but an in-store PROFIT CENTER; a scaled-down version of a stand-alone shipping center designed to meet self-storage space and labor limitations.

EVER GET ASKED IF YOU KNOW OF A GOOD MOVING SERVICE? Tell them about U-Pack®. Receive $75 for each referred customer that results in a U-Pack move. Plus, we'll give that customer a $25 discount. U-Pack will provide all marketing materials to get your program off the ground.

READY, SET, GROW INTO RECORDS MANAGEMENT. With O'Neil's state-of-the-art, competitively priced software (RS-SQL®), self-storage operators have all the tools they need to expand, profitably operate and successfully run a commercial record center.

Call us today
to *Make More Money*
877-622-5508

1/2 Hour FREE Consultation
Offer expires 12/31/09

Coast-To-Coast Storage, 533 Muirfield Dr, Atlantis FL 33462
www.askrk.com email: rk@askrk.com

Mail-In Cash Rebate

$5

Purchase the second edition "How to Make *MORE* Money in Self-Storage" and receive a $5 rebate. This book MUST be purchased on-line at www.h2mmm.com. Simply mail proof of purchase along with this coupon to:

533 Muirfield Dr.
Atlantis, FL 33462
Attn: Rebate Dept.

Effective through 12/31/09
One rebate per book purchased.
For rebate details go to www.h2mmm.com/rebate.html

Made in the USA
Lexington, KY
05 January 2010